*A transformational guide to trusting
yourself, building confidence, and creating
your most fulfilling life.*

Leslie Gilbert

Typesetting and cover design by Arjan van Woensel
ISBN paperback: 979-8-9873063-2-1
ISBN e-book: 979-8-9873063-0-7
ISBN audiobook: 979-8-9873063-1-4
First Edition

Dedication

*To those brave enough to seek the truth and
let their results be their guide.*

Table of Contents

Part 4: Liberation

Part 5: Exploration

Preface

Experts understand that results matter. Regardless of the topic, situation or circumstance, your results let you know exactly where you are. They also give you a starting point for change and the direction you need to move in. "Results matter" is a philosophy of change. How well you can apply and integrate this philosophy is determined by your fortitude and by your willingness to open and shift.

I've spent thousands of hours and tens of thousands of dollars on my own wellness journey. I've gotten lost in many pitfalls along the way. I've returned to those who offered me wisdom and advice even though I had initially considered them to be crazy. I learned that many of those people were in fact truth-tellers. I was able to shift my thinking because I'm a curious questioner of all things life and because I remained open-minded. I accepted my results regardless of my feelings around the outcomes. In other words, I most definitely learned things the hard way!

This book has lived in my head for well over five years. While I knew it was needed, my own fears almost kept it from becoming a reality. The world is full of naysayers—people who would rather attack and avoid versus open and expand. It's easy to attack people going against the status quo, a.k.a. the collective comfort zone. But nothing changes in the comfort zone. You get to avoid any underlying emotional issues when you stay in that zone and you go along to get along.

Some people will find this book to be a breath of fresh air; others won't. And that's okay! I wrote this book for everyone who's doing all the status-quo things, following all the rules, taking mainstream advice...and yet can't quite get where they want to be. This book is for the open-minded and those who believe in limitless potential. It's for the people who are listening and watching the world and thinking, "This can't be right."

With that in mind, I wrote this book as a time- and money-saving guide for you to help yourself. Everything in this book comes from my direct experience, study and practice. Read the book, do the work and open your mind. You can come back to these pages again and again and peel them back layer after layer to help you get to where you want to go: a state of being content and fulfilled. If I can do it, you can do it.

Having said that, it's much easier to see and understand a situation when you're not in the middle of it. Sometimes we need help—someone who can point us in a particular direction or help us see our blind spots. (For example, have your parents or friends ever known that the person you were dating wasn't good for you, but you couldn't see it?) Because this is a mindset book meant to guide you through making shifts in your thinking and your awareness, my hope is that reading these chapters will help you know how to ask questions, evaluate information and critically evaluate results in any given situation. That will make it less cumbersome to find someone who can help you, and you'll also be better equipped to avoid some pit-falls along the way.

Any person you trust with helping you must be a guide, not a dictator. You want someone who can ask you tough questions that will make you reflect—you *don't* want someone who will just say what they think you want to hear. Those "helpers" will only make things harder for you and keep you searching outside of yourself for answers, so choose your help wisely!

A word to the wise: there are no shortcuts. There is no great big giant central secret. If there were, I would tell you. If you want something other than what you have, then:

- You must open your mind.
- You must accept 100% responsibility for your life.
- You must let your results be your guide.
- You must question everything and then evaluate and integrate what you discover as needed.
- You must deal with your unresolved emotions and traumas.
- You must take care of your mind, body and spirit

by surrounding yourself with the highest-quality people and nourishment you can find.

I wish you nothing but wellness, dear reader.

Big love and many thanks,

Leslie Gilbert

June 8, 2022

Introduction:
This is for you!

Somewhere along the way, we have given up our power and our control over how we live. We have outsourced our decision-making. We trust people who don't know us at all to tell us what to do, how to live our lives and what to believe. We don't even bother to question the things that are confusing. We go along to get along. We have children, but we only take some of the responsibility for them. We date, marry and partner with people we don't communicate with and then get furious when we are unfulfilled. Often, we didn't even choose these people— our families, friends and what society deems a "good mate" selected them for us. We suffer needlessly.

The mission of this book is simple: I want you to completely and totally know with your whole self—your mind, body and spirit—that *you are the expert of your life and you are 100% responsible for it.*

I am inviting you to reclaim power over yourself and your life. I am offering this information with the permission of your heart. I am serving as a guide. My role is to ask you questions and show you a way back to regaining expert status within your own life. I'll be walking you through evaluating information and encouraging you to listen to your gut. I will *not* be telling you what to do with your life. *You are the expert.*

This is a choose-your-own-adventure experience. At any time, the choice is yours: to do, be, practice, consider, question, integrate and learn. At any time, you can slow down, stop or speed up. I trust you to make the best decisions for yourself. While we might have the same destination of true wellness in mind, we each have our own decisions to make while traveling the path.

I realized during the crazy time of Covid (which started in the U.S. in the spring of 2020) that I knew almost no one who played the leading role in their own life. Have you ever watched an action movie and thought of yourself as the person who would run towards danger, like William Wallace in *Braveheart*? Or King Leonidas in *300* when he roared into battle? Remember, *he required no one to follow him*. He simply plunged ahead because he knew it was the right thing to do.

Even before Covid hit, I had witnessed an outsourcing of decision-making. People were continuously looking to someone else to tell them what was best. Even the people I had formerly viewed as living authentically were swept away in a wave of virtue signaling. They're still caught up in that wave now.

It's important to note: virtue signaling does not equal authenticity. True leaders and experts don't virtue-signal. They're too busy living their talk and walking their walk. They simply go first because they're independent. Tragically, despite a few sterling examples of true leaders, independent thought is severely lacking in the world today.

To live authentically is to realize that you are the expert. *That* is the power. Realizing you're the expert is also what it means to be a leader. You can't be the leader of your own life if you aren't willing to be the expert of it.

It's time to decide for yourself if you want to become the leader of your own life! Carefully consider the following questions. Give yourself some time to read them uninterrupted and see what comes up for you:

- Are you interested in living as the expert of your life?
- Do you believe you're the expert of your life in every situation?
- Have you considered where/when you give your power away?
- Do you even want that power?
- Are you ready?
- Is this the right time?
- Are you able to commit to bringing change into your life?
- Do you think you're 100% responsible for your life?
- Do you consider yourself to be healthy, open-minded and curious?

If you're having trouble answering these questions *and* you aren't completely open to self-exploration, you might consider donating this book, because the timing might not be right for you to continue. Reclaiming expert status is a rocky road, yet totally worth it! If you *are* still with me, grab a notebook and pen and turn the page.

PART 1

EVOLUTION

Story

"The moment you change your perception is the moment you rewrite the chemistry of your body."
– Bruce H. Lipton, Ph.D.

"So, Leslie, how did you get here?" you might be asking. That is a very long story—a tedious tale of tears, heartache, disappointment, swear words, an endless number of bad days and so many symptoms of illness. While my personal story is vital and is the origin story for this book, I'm going to give you the short version. Why? Because how you talk about yourself is a key concept when it comes to dealing with mindset as well as healing. How you talk about past events in your life—and whether or not you relive the emotions from those events—reflects your state of mind. How you describe yourself and the labels you adopt also reflect your state of mind.

If I've learned anything over the last two decades, it's that there is more than one way to heal no matter what exactly you're healing. I'm not going to lay out my detailed methodology for healing because it might work for you and it might not. That's the thing about people—for all the ways we're the same, we're also different, and our life experiences as well as our beliefs *all* factor into how we heal (or don't). *You heal you. What you believe is what you get.*

A well-lived life takes place in the present. While my past may hold defining moments, I am not defined *by* them. The universe has conspired to bring together my experiences, training, education, practice and personal wisdom in the form of this book. Let me tell you a little bit about that synergy.

I used to be a rule-follower. I did what was expected and I

believed that hard work would pay off. The problem was that no matter what I did, I was a day late and a dollar short. I couldn't understand why things were working out for other people but not for me. I did have some success, yes, but I reached a plateau very quickly. I was always missing something that would have gotten me to the next level…or so others told me.

I was watching people with less education who had a crappy work ethic and a generally unpleasant demeanor win at life. At least, "winning" in the way that society traditionally defines success. My agreement with this definition set me up for failure because I was *never* enough regardless of my effort, dedication, talent, intelligence and loyalty.

I began to realize that I had deeply-ingrained senses of obligation and performance as defined by someone else and that many people I knew were actually *not* "successful." A few were—I knew a handful of people who were making their own rules and living a life of contentment. But they were in the minority. I'm talking about the majority of people I knew, myself included. (Most people are very unhappy even though they look happy from the outside.)

We were all living in fear of what others would think of us or which relationships would be lost if we chose to do what our hearts actually desired. Realizing this was a wake-up call for me. I was finally beginning to understand something about the world that had never quite sat right with me, something I really couldn't articulate. Although I didn't know it at the time, this realization would set me on a course that would blow up everything I thought was true and open me up to a world I couldn't have even fathomed.

Hindsight is, as they say, 20/20. Nowadays, I am *so* grateful for having those feelings of not fitting in! I am so grateful I kept thinking, "There has to be something more!" Those feelings propelled me into the adventure of a lifetime, and it's ongoing.

Fast-forward a bit... I was a college graduate with three degrees and a well-rounded work history. I was a member of the twice-divorced club now living in a committed relationship. I was also restless and unfulfilled. I was discussing the monotony of chores and the daily grind with a family member when she told me, "This is it!" She explained that there was nothing else. I should decide soon if I wanted kids, she told me, and because I wasn't getting any younger.

Her words hit me hard. I mean, seriously… What the hell was that!? I was in my early thirties! After the initial shock, I thought, "Wait a minute—you mean my purpose in life is to be beaten down by chores and have kids and just suck it all up because that's life?" My immediate response to that thought was "NO! That can't be right!" Right then and there, I decided that path would *not* be my life.

In the years that followed, I slowly started experiencing various general symptoms: fatigue, low energy, agitation, difficult periods, having a short fuse, sleep issues, chronic systemic inflammation, seasonal allergies, etc. Most people attribute that kind of slow accumulation of symptoms to aging, but I knew in my heart that belief was a limiting one. Plenty of people didn't experience aging that way at all. What did those people know that I didn't? What could they be doing (or not doing) that I wasn't? I had never been sick often in the past, and the only prescription drug I was taking was birth control.

I diligently followed the standard recommendation to have yearly check-ups with a gynecologist. (After all, that's the only way to get birth control pills.) My doctor did the requisite lab work and exams and asked if I was having any problems. After hearing about my symptoms, she prescribed a drug used to treat heavy bleeding related to difficult periods. Shortly after beginning that medication, I thought I was having a stroke—I was having trouble finding words and I struggled to speak in complete sentences. Something wasn't right. I stopped taking that medication immediately.

Still, every year, I went to my annual appointment. Every year, my symptoms got worse. The doctor prescribed antibiotics because I *might* have an infection I didn't know about even though I didn't have any symptoms that would suggest an infection. I had more tests and an ultrasound. I was diagnosed with more conditions. I experienced even more signs of illness. When I asked about other possible explanations for what I was experiencing or the root cause, the doctor yelled at me for questioning her. She'd never even heard of the information I was asking about, even though, that information might have explained my symptoms. It was clear to me that she didn't know the answers to my questions and didn't like being questioned.

My doctor continued to encourage me to take various prescriptions to manage my symptoms. She practically begged me to get a Mirena® intrauterine device. Her anger and insistence were so unsettling to me that I felt sure she was receiving some sort of monetary benefit from what she was recommending. That had me questioning her trustworthiness. She obviously believed that anything wrong with me could be fixed by taking prescriptions and/or undergoing procedures.

After taking thyroid medication under her supervision and seeing little improvement, I was referred to an endocrinologist. My lab work indicated continued issues and a need for increased doses to treat hypothyroidism. I have five paternal relatives and a sibling with thyroid conditions, so I was well-versed in genetic thyroid conditions. I had started my own research to discover the root cause of my symptoms as well as how to heal them.

After submitting to the endocrinologist's round of testing, I was told I had prediabetes along with hypothyroidism. Just like the gynecologist had said, the endocrinologist told me that continued medication would solve my problems. My symptoms actually were somewhat remedied in the first month of taking an increased dose of the medication. But then all of my symptoms returned…and with increased intensity.

I was scheduled to see the endocrinologist again in six months, so I went on a deep dive of research and applying what I learned. I was also reading *One Second After* by William R. Forstchen. The novel deals with an unexpected electromagnetic pulse attack on the United States. A character in the story dies because she can no longer get her insulin due to the dystopian conditions. That got me thinking: what if something happened and I couldn't get my thyroid medication? What if my prediabetes progressed to diabetes? Would I die because of it? Would I (could I) live but be miserable? None of that appealed to me in any way, shape or form. I started digging a little deeper.

After six months had passed, I'd come to believe that hypothyroidism was a misdiagnosis and that lifestyle changes would fix my symptoms. I was determined to prove that to the endocrinologist. Fortunately for me, he was an old-school kind of doctor and up for a good old-fashioned experiment. We came up with a plan to wean me off the prescription. I would apply my research and come back in six months. The doctor gave me a diet to follow along with some other recommendations, but I didn't follow his advice. I chose to listen to my gut—I knew he was wrong.

~

Note: Did you know that not all doctors/laboratories use the same information to interpret results? In the example of prediabetes, I asked a nurse from another doctor's office about my lab work. She told me that in her office, prediabetes wasn't a thing—no one from that office would have even made a big deal out of the those results. That applies to all lab work, by the way. While there may be "standards," you're essentially relying on one person's interpretation of those standards.

~

So, how did all of this turn out? After taking medication for about a year and gaining twelve pounds (even though systemic inflammation made it look like I had gained fifty) *and* experiencing increasing symptoms, I found out I did not have hypothyroidism or prediabetes. But I'm jumping ahead a bit...

When I went back to see the endocrinologist, he asked me how I'd been. I told him about all the ways my symptoms had improved. I also told him that I'd been working hard to prove my misdiagnosis. He said, "I guess we'll see." I said, "I guess we will." When my lab work came back *not* indicating prediabetes or a thyroid condition, he reluctantly told me that yes, I had been misdiagnosed. He clearly did not enjoy the moment and said I'd have to come back every year for a check-up. When I asked him why, he said, "Just to make sure." I said, "Okay." When I left his office, I declined to schedule another appointment. I have not been and won't be back to see him.

I tell you this story to illustrate how imperative it is to understand that lab work, scans and other diagnostic tools are snapshots in time. They do not indicate that a condition, symptom or illness is set in stone. You might consider how often these tests can be and are wrong.

Let's say you're on the way to a doctor's appointment. There's a wreck on the highway that puts you behind schedule. Once you do arrive, there's no parking spot in sight. You eventually find a place to park and race into the office. You're given paperwork to complete, but you're called back before you're done. As soon as you're in the exam room, a nurse takes your vitals.

The likelihood that your blood pressure is elevated in this scenario is high because it's a perfectly normal bodily response. Using that snapshot to determine that you have consistent high blood pressure and need medication is completely inappropriate—your blood pressure is *supposed* to rise in times of stress, worry and anxiety. Unfortunately, the way healthcare workers take and use blood pressure readings often does not account for this normal bodily response. I'm sure you've never been asked any questions about what happened right before that appointment or about any other concerns you might have that could be creating chronic stress and ensuing elevated blood pressure. And then there's "white coat syndrome," which is extreme anxiety in dealing with medical professionals in any capacity. Anyone with this syndrome will have elevated blood pressure when dealing with doctors.

Getting back to my case, a misdiagnosed thyroid condition meant that I unnecessarily took medication for a year. That did not strike me as the path to wellness. In fact, my misdiagnosis formed the basis for a philosophy that I call "results matter." Sure, I could have continued taking the medication. I could have added more prescriptions to manage my symptoms and the side effects/symptoms of the other medications. But I wasn't getting better! I was getting *worse*. And so I chose to listen to my gut instinct and move forward accordingly. That experience also taught me that *I* am the expert when it comes to Leslie.

Granted, living as the expert of yourself is often easier said than done, in large part because the path to wellness isn't a straight line. You will revisit things you thought you were done with and learn even more about yourself. There is an undoing, an unlearning that has to happen so that you can accept yourself as you *were* and who you *are*. You also need to unlearn some things so that you can have hope for who you might *become*. This path is messy as hell! It is, however, the only way to truly be yourself and have the freedom to design your life as you want it to be.

Interestingly, even though I had the realization that *I* am the expert of my life, I went right back to that same gynecologist even though alarm bells were ringing everywhere. After my annual exam, the nurse called and bluntly told me that I had cancer. I had a complete and total meltdown. I proceeded to get very drunk and did a lot of ugly crying. I was terrified. My fear had reached such a level that when my husband got home from work, I could barely say the word "cancer."

Thankfully, my husband has a pretty zen personality. He told me not to worry and he reminded me that we'd learned there's a root cause to disease (which is really dis-ease or a lack of ease) and that we would find it and deal with it. That included cancer, he pointed out.

I did follow up with my doctor to get her advice on how to proceed. Her first recommendation was surgery to remove multiple organs. In the midst of being terrified, I remember thinking, "Why the hell is this the *first* response? Why not do another round of tests to confirm her diagnosis? What about a second opinion? What about alternative, natural approaches to cancer treatment?" Why not anything *else* first, really, before removal of my organs?

I started asking questions. Her responses were less than acceptable. She started backpedaling, saying, "Maybe we should do some other things before surgery." I told her I wanted to think about things and I would be in touch.

Mind you, even before the C-word was thrown around, I'd been very unwell. Sometimes, my symptoms were so bad that I couldn't get out of bed or leave the house. I lost many, many days to dealing with symptoms. I cried rivers of tears; I screamed countless times; I was worried, anxious and living in fear.

But then I had figured out how to deal with those symptoms. When I trusted my gut instincts, I had the experience of healing something many had said couldn't be healed. And so I kept reminding myself that I know what's best for me.

What happened next isn't for the faint of heart or devotees of modern medicine. It isn't for people who prefer to submit to authority, people who have surrendered their critical thinking and decision-making skills to someone else. It isn't for anyone who doesn't want to take responsibility for and *be* the expert of their own life.

I ghosted that doctor completely.

No phone call. No follow-up. No answer to the certified mail sent my way. No "official" treatment for cancer at all.

I only ever discuss what I call the "cancer scare" rarely and vaguely. Because that's exactly what the doctor's office did: scare me. Every interaction with them was fueled by fear; their's and mine. I'm not a fan of "the fight against cancer" battle cry or the organizations and businesses that are making a profit from that fight. I do not accept what the majority of people accept as the truth when it comes to treating cancer.

I did not share my cancer diagnosis with anyone but my husband until the last few years because I didn't want people treating me like I was already dead. I didn't want to have to deal with/process other people's beliefs and fears on the subject. They did not know what I knew. They had not healed themselves and proved a misdiagnosis. They did not consider information, resources and knowledge that were outside of the mainstream. Misery loves company, and that misery includes fear. I knew that if I told anyone about my diagnosis, they would say, "Better safe than sorry."

∼

If I've done a good job of telling you my story, you should

be feeling uncomfortable and have some questions at this point. I'll try to answer some of them. In the case of my misdiagnosis of hypothyroidism, it's important to recognize a few things: 1) Western medicine says that hypothyroidism can't be cured, only managed. It is diagnosed via lab tests. 2) My misdiagnosis was only confirmed because I did my own research and questioned everything presented to me by two different doctors. 3) In terms of my diagnosis, Western medicine in the form of the test and the doctor interpreting the test was wrong.

You might be saying, "Well, if the first test was wrong, then the second one could be wrong, too." My answer to that is "Exactly!" How many people are managing symptoms via prescription drugs and lab work rather than getting to their root of their issues and changing their lifestyle? What unnecessary extra burdens have been placed on their bodies, wallets and vitality, burdens they may have avoided had they only asked some questions and trusted themselves?

In the case of my cancer diagnosis, all of the above applies, but with the following caveat: Western medicine operates under the assumption that without treatment, cancer will kill you. But mainstream medicine simply isn't correct when it comes to my story. I'm now healthier, not sicker. If I'd listened to that doctor without question, I would have had organs removed and gone through toxic, poisonous treatments and hoped for the best. I also would have been trapped in a fear spiral and/or on the treatment train for the rest of my life, waiting and wondering if each trip to the doctor would tell me that the cancer was back. That is not life. It is suffering.

Thankfully, I've learned that closed minds operate in closed systems. And that hope and critical thinking are not part of closed systems. Here's the best part: we all have a choice in the matter. We can all choose whether to be closed or to be open.

Your takeaway...

Doctors are people, and people aren't perfect and/or all-knowing.

Out of the book into your life...

Set a timer for 10 to 15 minutes.

Consider any part of your life where you rely on someone with a certain degree, title, designation, license, etc. Jot that down. Now, review each person and why you are relying on them. Are you getting the results you want from each person? Write down "Yes" or "No" and the reasons why. Do you blindly accept what they say no matter what, even if your gut feeling tells you otherwise?

When it comes to medical matters, have you considered how many people are on medication as a result of a faulty test? Have you thought about how many people have ignored their gut instincts and continued taking medication that did not resolve their symptoms?

Next, compare what you know about how Western Medicine treats emergencies/trauma/accidents versus symptoms/conditions/diseases. Have you ever given much thought to the differences? Which gets the better results? Is it possible for you to utilize what Western Medicine excels at and look for other solutions for everything else? Why or Why not?

Lessons

"If you are not willing to learn, no one can help you. If you are determined to learn, no one can stop you."
– Zig Ziglar

For approximately a year after my last appointment with my doctor, I was bombarded with phone calls and letters. All with the insistence that I must contact them and get treated or that if I didn't want treatment at their office to please provide the name of the doctor I was seeing. My response was silence. This was someone covering their ass, not someone interested in my well-being.

In case you aren't aware, the medical community must follow certain standards of care. By law, there are things they must say and/or do. Patients, generally speaking, get the exact same treatment plans for whatever ails them. *But* no medical authority knows exactly how any treatment will affect a given person. Most healthcare workers don't ask enough questions to understand each person's individual circumstances that will directly affect whether or not any treatment will work. Results are not the guide in medical world. Health and well-being are not the goals of the medical world.

Disease, illness and sickness are big business. The 2021 Hulu hit *Dopesick* portrays the real events involving a pharmaceutical company flat-out lying and manipulating data (aided by a federal agency) to increase their bottom line. Pediatricians earn millions of dollars annually just from following the vaccine schedule. If you think there isn't a monetary basis underpinning what medical professionals tell you, you're wrong.

The biggest takeaway from my own story is that *results*

matter. You need to know how to make that happen for your story, too, which means you need to know how to evaluate information and results. Regardless of the subject at hand, if you aren't getting the results you want, then consider that to be a flashing neon sign telling you to make a change.

My story illustrates how I was able to reclaim my expert status through health challenges. You can, however, reclaim the leading role of expert in your life from any place or situation—the same lessons apply. Just know that true wellness won't ever be yours unless you first accept that *you* are responsible for your life. Taking full responsibility is living the business of being *you*.

Lesson 1: *You are the expert.*
You already have everything you need. You only have to learn how to see and use your inner wisdom.

Lesson 2: *Find and heal the root cause of your difficulties.*
All of your efforts will just be Band-Aids until you address the root cause of what's going on.

Lesson 3: *Learn how your body works.*

I'm floored at how little we understand about how our own bodies work.

Lesson 4: *Inspiration can happen anytime, anywhere, from anything.*
For me, a novel about a dystopian future prompted me to ask questions I wouldn't have considered otherwise.

Lesson 5: *Deal with unresolved emotions and traumas.*
This is directly tied to Lesson 2. The two lessons are interrelated. Every symptom, disease, condition and diagnosis at a minimum has an emotional component. In most cases, *not* dealing with your emotions caused whatever you're dealing with physically.

Lesson 6: *There's no one way to heal, whatever you're healing.*
You will find an endless number of people, places and solutions. You will be open to things when you are ready for them. It's important to note that *you heal you!* Everything else is either supporting that goal or preventing you from reaching it. Remember, results matter.

Lesson 7: *In your own way and in your own time.*

No one else can do what you need to do for you. If they suggest they can, run! Your mindset is the most important factor. You need to stay open so that whatever you need finds its way to you. Cultivate an open mind and enable yourself to explore, change, adapt, integrate, grow and expand.

Lesson 8: *You must live your life in your way, even if doing so disappoints someone.*
That may mean you won't take over the family business after all or that you will or won't get married. That may mean you will or won't have kids or will or won't attend college. In short, living your life in your own way means you won't blindly just do anything that someone *else* thinks you should do but that *you* don't want to do. You won't adhere to someone else's idea of what life should be. Leaders go first, my friend, even when it's hard and unpopular...even when going first might be perceived as a little crazy. It's necessary, though, because living a life that isn't aligned with your mind, body and spirit is the definition of fighting against nature.

How you explore these lessons will uniquely shape your path. Although we may share similar experiences, feelings and beliefs, we are all individuals with individual experiences. What and how you choose to do, be, explore, practice and integrate will provide your results. None of this is a one-size-fits-all process. It's a "What fits me?" kind of process. There are many steps and many levels… and the process will go on throughout your entire life.

Your takeaway...

Lessons are only lessons if you apply what you learned.

Out of the book into your life...

Is there a time when you thought you had learned a lesson but you nonetheless continued to find yourself in the same old pattern or situation?

What does applying a lesson and what you learned from that lesson mean to you?

Can you think of a time when you said to yourself "Lesson learned"? What made you so sure? What factors were at play that made you realize you would not repeat the same actions?

What emotions did you feel when you thought you had learned the lesson and then what emotions did you feel when you later realized you hadn't learned the lesson?

PART 2

FOUNDATION

Philosophy

"What you think, you become. What you feel, you attract.
What you imagine, you create."
– Buddha

One of my favorite ways to learn is by listening to podcasts. There's so much we can learn from hearing someone's voice and how they talk about their work and personal life as well as how they answer questions. At the end of each episode, Dave Asprey of *Bulletproof Radio* always asks guests the same question: if they could only tell people three things they could do to improve their health, wellness and longevity, what would those three things be?

When I listened to Asprey's podcast and heard that question, it intrigued me. By then, I had spent quite a few years healing a variety of my own health conditions. I wondered what would I say. I decided my three recommendations would be mindset, movement and real food. Let's explore each one of those.

Mindset

Am I open to receive, or am I closed off/contracted in fear?

Having an open mind creates endless possibilities. Opening your mind and keeping it open is the greatest gift you can give yourself. That's how you can heal, blast through obstacles and dissolve limiting beliefs. Having an open mind gives you what you need to move forward on your path, because then what you need will find you. When you open your mind, you open doors; when you change your mind, you change your life.

Movement

Am I moving towards something? Am I exercising, training and moving my body? Is my energy moving, or is it stagnant?

For many people, movement is the easiest of the three factors, at least at the beginning. The more you do, the more you *can* do. Moving is the quickest way to improve how you feel. Our bodies are designed to move! Sedentary lifestyles are a main factor in disease. Exercising, moving and training daily is vital to enjoying good health. Know that your body is a reflection of your mind and vice versa. Anything unresolved—your worries, traumas, disappointments, etc.—are reflected in your body in some way. Those negative mindsets can be seen in your posture, heard in your voice, contained in your tissues and so on. Emotions are energy, and energy is never lost—it's only transformed. When you move your body, you change your mind.

Movement is also the direction of your energy, focus and attention. Are you in living in the past, present or future? Where is your mind most of the day? Do you often relive something from long ago (focused on the past) or are you worried/anxious about something that hasn't happened yet (focused on the future)? What if you focused on the people right in front of you *right now*? What if you directed your energy to the present moment? Think about how different your life might be if your attention was primarily focused on the now, if you healed the wounds from your past and planned for the future as best you can, yet stayed open to how those plans will play out.

Real food

What am I consuming? Is it nourishing? Is it building me up? Is it helpful?

This factor comes down to a fundamental shift in thinking, namely that food is fuel. It's not entertainment; it's not a reward. What you put into your body contributes to how you feel—i.e., whether you're lively and energetic or agitated and depressed. Your choice of fuel helps determine the quality of your cells. Your body generates millions of new cells daily. Where do you think it's getting the energy and material to do that?

There are innumerable diets and food plans that you could follow, but my recommendation is simple: always consume the highest-quality foods you can afford that are as close to nature as possible. That means whole foods as you would find them in nature, not in a package.

Over the years, I've expanded my definition of what "real food" is. Initially, I thought it was all about what people eat and drink. Now I realize that "real food" also includes the company we keep, what we read, what we watch on television and what we choose to listen to, from shows on streaming services to news sources. These things can be nourishing or damaging. We consume all of this just like we consume the food we eat. Bottom line: you can't build a healthy body on candy *or* on low-vibe, closed-off people, situations or entertainment.

Mindset, movement and real food are what I used to heal myself from a plethora of symptoms, challenges and conditions. These three spokes form the wheel of my philosophy, which is that results matter.

Why results matter

If you aren't getting what you want, it's time to make a change! By using mindset, movement and real food, you can address any difficulty or challenge you're experiencing. Your results are your guide. That means taking an honest look at yourself and your life. It means it's time for a pattern interrupt. Then you need to get your mind right and simplify your life.

How does this philosophy of "results matter" relate to wellness? Wellness is made up of more than just your physical health—wellness covers multiple aspects of your life. These aspects are really about your relationships. How do you interact with/relate to money, other people, health, fun, spirituality, emotions, purpose and your physical living/working spaces? *True wellness* is an ongoing, dynamic process of change and growth. It's not just about living without symptoms, conditions or illness. True wellness is a complete, whole state of being well that encompasses your entire life.

Some aspects of your life will feel easy; others will feel challenging. I'd like to introduce you to (what I call) "The Five Challenges" you need to consider: physical stress, chemical stress, emotional stress, toxicity and deficiency. If you're struggling with or overwhelmed by something in your life, it's typically a result of one (or more) of these five categories.

Physical stress can be the result of…

… broken bones, pulled hamstrings, hitting your funny bone, the state of your home/car/office, the arrangement/quality of furniture and décor, soft tissue injury/pain, joint discomfort, chronic pain, any diagnosis from a medical professional, etc.

Chemical stress can be the result of…

… medications, legal/illegal drugs, alcohol, pesticides, stings from wasps or bees, strong scents from perfume and cologne and cleaning products, vitamins, supplements, the food you eat/don't eat, etc.

Emotional stress can be the result of…

… the death of a loved one, a difficult boss, arguing with your kids/spouse, low-vibe people, drama queens and kings, negative Nancies, naysayers, worry, over thinking, anxiety, depression, chronic pain, difficult friends and in-laws, owning a business, physical injuries and more.

Toxicity can be the result of…

… too much of anything that causes an adverse response from your system, highly charged emotional relationships, pesticides that affect what stress hormones are released and when and for how long, chemicals and other ingredients that act as hormone disruptors (or even pseudo estrogens) that confuse your body's natural systems and create a multitude of symptoms, heavy metals stored in your body's fat and cells and other tissues, etc.

Deficiency can be the result of…

… lack of nutrition, not getting your needs and wants met, a lack of connection and or purpose in life, anything that contributes to physical, chemical and emotional stresses, etc.

≈

Note: "Stress" as discussed here refers to a chronic negative state in your mind, body and/or spirit. There's more than one kind of stress. Some stress is considered positive and good—that's known as "eustress." But when it's negative and bad, it's "distress." Ongoing, negative stress is chronic stress.

~

Once you've categorized your challenges and issues, you've taken the first step to resolving them. You might find it a helpful to know that various kinds of stresses can fall into more than one category. For example, there's typically a bodily response (i.e., physical stress) to emotional stress—you may have poor posture, rounding/hunching of shoulders and/or pain.

Also know that what stresses out one person isn't necessarily going to be a stressor for someone else. Each of us deals with difficulty in our own way, filtered through our own personal experiences. When you've been arguing with your spouse, maybe a walk can help you clear your mind and give you space. However, if you're grieving the loss of a loved one, a walk might not help you process the loss. You may find that instead you need additional sleep so that you have plenty of brainpower to navigate through the steps of grief.

In my case, the moment I realized that any situation, problem, challenge, illness, difficulty, etc. fell into one or more of these five categories, that knowledge simplified things and made me feel like I could handle anything.

That said, The Five Challenges are filled with subtlety and nuance. *The key is breaking down your challenges into manageable parts.* Then you can discover the root cause of the obstacle, implement the philosophy of results matter and begin healing. Trust yourself and take the lead! And remember that the path to wellness isn't a line—it's more like a spiral. You'll continue to revisit things, round and round, until they're cleared.

Embracing the philosophy of results matter will move you closer to true wellness. And any time your results aren't what you desired, you can revisit mindset, movement, real food and The Five Challenges and reengage with those results.

Your takeaway...

Your results are your guide.

Out of the book into your life...

Have you ever taken a job only to realize that the work environment wasn't a good fit for you? How did you handle the situation?

Have you ever tried to learn a new skill or hobby only to find that you were making little progress? Before giving up, did you consider finding another teacher? Did you consider reaching out to someone else with that skill/talent/hobby and asking questions?

Think about your relationships. Are they one-sided?

Where in your life have you let your results be your guide? Where have you ignored your results? When have you gotten poor results but continued to do the same things?

Take 5 minutes to make a list of the areas of your life

that you feel are hard, overwhelming or challenging.
Then categorize those areas according to the five
aspects. We will return to this list later!

Integrity

"Congruency is your currency."
– Gracie Jurkowski

Now that we've simplified life's challenges, let's get to the heart of the lesson. As you move forward, keep in mind that "simple" is easy in theory and often difficult in practice. That's because each of us is the product of our particular upbringing, experiences, education, culture, region, jobs/career and more. This means while people can be similar, our perspectives aren't the same. What's troublesome for one is easy for another. Negative experiences can be one person's bad day and another's inspiration.

Although we're each very unique, we still bury ourselves in the expectations, obligations, advice and opinions of other people. Of course life feels hard or even scary! Everything you do, say, think or want gets put through the filter of other people instead of yourself. This makes you grow increasingly sad and resentful, not to mention anxious and angry.

Congruency is the state or quality of being in agreement/harmony with yourself. Your internal state may be consistent but is it congruent? Currency is a medium of exchange. Is your predominant state of being harmonious and peaceful or is it something else? Are you able to say that congruency is your currency, meaning that your interactions with others reflect an internal harmony? Integrity is the quality or state of being complete, whole and sound in moral principle, honesty and sincerity. Is that truly how you show up for yourself and your life? Congruency and integrity go hand in hand.

Too many people have outsourced their responsibilities

and decision-making skills. When this happens, we are no longer the experts in our own lives. Instead, we become victims. Victims blame others and circumstances whenever the results they get aren't the results they want. Victimhood is a chronic state of being. Victims either look for solutions outside of themselves or they don't look for a solution at all.

How does one avoid victimhood? Here's where the idea that *you already have everything you need* should kick in. Experts already know what to do, right? That's why they're experts. So look in the mirror and say "Hello!" Get reacquainted with your inner expert.

Go back to your list of what's challenging you, the one that you categorized by The Five Challenges. Circle the top two or three things that would make you feel like you're moving forward if you were to address them. This should take no more than 10 to 30 seconds. Let your instincts kick in! Decisions made, exercise done. If you weren't able to choose two or three things, jot down the thoughts that popped up for you. Maybe the list has turned into a paralyzing exercise in indecision. No problem—all that means is that your starting place is a little different. In that case, reflect on the first thought you had as you were frozen in indecision. Keep asking yourself questions and answering honestly until you've discovered the underlying fear.

Time to get down to the business of being yourself! And be truthful about things. Many of us were raised to be good and polite even when we felt like *not* being good or polite. That mentality can lead to putting everyone else before ourselves. It teaches us that it's more important to do or say whatever makes everyone else comfortable rather than to do or say what we *actually* want.

But to be clear, I'm not advocating a do or say anything we want, anywhere, anytime mentality. The opposite of the anything, anytime mindset is to cultivate discernment. According to *Webster's*, discernment is "the power of keen perception or judgment; insight; acumen." To be discerning is "having or showing good judgment or understanding; astute." In order to have the power of keen judgment and insight you must embrace your true self and use the knowledge gained through that journey to develop discernment. Consider the following...

- When do you say "Yes" when you mean "No" and

vice versa?

- When do you go along to get along?
- When you need help, do you ask for it?
- Do you often manipulate situations so that you get to be the martyr? Martyrs are still victims—it's just self-inflicted victimhood.
- What is challenging for you? Do you explore your challenges? Do you look for ways to improve how you deal with difficulties, or do you look for ways that those difficulties are someone else's fault? Do you focus on and incessantly repeat (inside and out loud) negative statements?
- What things, people, situations, words, etc. agitate you and bring up anger, sadness and other negative emotions?
- What brings up positive emotions like joy, happiness, excitement, passion and love?
- Does exploring any of this feel terrifying? If it does, what might that mean?

Growing and expanding as a person isn't an easy path—in fact, much of the time, it can feel terrifying. But the quickest way to deal with fear is to just go right on through! Explore, adjust, accept and learn the lessons. Sure, it'd be so much easier to outsource everything and sit on your high horse and say it's someone else's fault, but that won't get you anywhere. You aren't able to discern if you're angry or resentful or experiencing negativity.

Being the expert of your life means that your mind, body and spirit are in sync. Being the expert means that you are self-aware. You know what you want; you know your core values and where your lines of acceptance begin and end.

But before we dig into how you can go about reclaiming expert status, you should know about the fakers. Fakers are people who give the illusion of taking care of themselves despite the fact that in reality, they're avoiding the very real work that would give them confidence in their lives and instead are covering up that lack with bravado. Don't be a faker.

True experts:

- Aren't passive-aggressive.
- Aren't rigid, closed-minded or closed off.
- Don't say things like "This is who I am. You can take it or leave it!"

- Also don't say "I'm a grown-ass man/woman!"
- Know the difference between power (a state of being that comes from within) and force (an act of violence).
- Lift people up instead of tearing them down.
- Don't align their lives to fear and scarcity.
- Aren't sitting around hoping their enemies will get what they deserve or become the target of some kind of karmic retribution.
- Understand voluntary cooperation over competition.
- Live their talk *and* understand the concept that *congruency is their currency.*

Looking at that list, can you say without hesitation and without a shred of a doubt that you're the expert of your life? My guess is no, and that's okay. That's why we're here!

Reclaiming expert status doesn't mean that you never look for guidance—after all, one person can't know everything there is to know about everything. But you *can* get clear on your core values. You *can* undo and unlearn all of the things you've layered over your own wants and needs, the stuff you've unwittingly taken on from other people. You *can* think critically when you encounter new information. You *can* do your own research, resolve conflicting beliefs within yourself and integrate what you've learned.

Your takeaway...

Congruency is your currency.

Out of the book and into your life...

Great news—you're on your way! Awareness is the key to change. You've also identified some challenge areas you'd like to improve. Now let's define your core values. Your core values are how you live your life; they form the basis for how you make decisions. They shape whether you view circumstances, situations and behaviors as being good or bad. Core values are the guiding force in your life.

Time to take out your notebook and pen! Or, feel free to

use this exercise as a meditation moment.

1. Write a short paragraph describing who you are, what you do and what's most important to you/what your top priorities in life are. If you completely remove what you do for a living, what's left? Have you set up your life so that all of your confidence and self-worth come from your job title? If you couldn't do that job tomorrow, would you still feel confident? Does the idea of *not* doing your job create any feelings of panic or negativity? What if you were to remove your family role? Say you're a parent. When your kids move out on their own, what will you do with your time? Do you have any hobbies or interests that are just yours and not tied up with any family members?

2. Consider times in your life when you felt the most confident, fulfilled, content, etc. See if you can bring those moments to mind. Then jot down what stands out to you. Who was there? Who wasn't? Is that relevant? Where were you? What were you doing? Was this for work or did

this happen during your personal life?

3. Identify five to ten core values that are the most important to you. Look at the examples below for some ideas. This list in not all-inclusive— please add to these as needed.

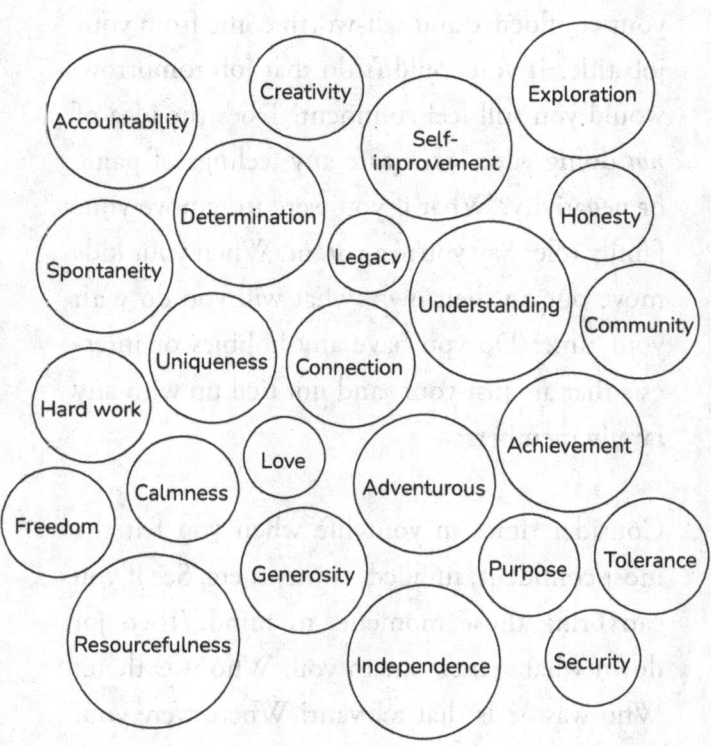

4. Reflect on this exercise. Where are your values, priorities and actions inconsistent? For example, are you working 80 hours a week but saying that family is the most important thing to you? Are you maxing out credit cards to keep up with your friends because you're afraid of what they might think of you, yet saying you want to save money? Are you living in a huge house despite hating housework and having to maintain a property?

5. Of those five to ten values you've already identified, choose your top three to five values. Through the lens of those values, evaluate how you make decisions and how you design your life. Do they fit? Do you need to make changes? Could you take a baby step to better align your life and values? What are you doing to ensure that you consider the future through these values versus falling back into your old ways of doing things?

Although this particular exercise is a huge and multi-faceted one, smaller steps can ease you into big changes. Some of you are "Rip the bandage off!" types and will want to do the big things all at once. That's fine, too. Remember, *you* are the expert! But if you're prone to thinking about everything that can go wrong, create an incremental plan. Know that you can take three or six or nine months or even a year to carry out that plan.

While I encourage stepping outside of your comfort zone, I don't think it would be best to blow up your life in a way that you might not be ready to deal with. Only *you* know the best way! As you gain confidence in reclaiming your power and aligning your life with your values, you will find that every decision and situation will become easier.

PART 3

TRANSFORMATION

Shift

*"The worst thing is watching someone drown and
not being able to convince them that
they can save themselves by just standing up."*
– Anonymous

From my story, we've seen an example of how a person might begin to reclaim their expert status, and by using The Five Challenges and the life philosophy of results matter, I've given you a framework to reflect on your own life. Now it's time to shift your mindset a little more. Open your mind and keep it open—it's time to examine *all* of your beliefs!

Shifting your mindset is going to require you to consider two things that feel painful to most folks: 1) Your beliefs might be wrong and 2) You don't know what you don't know.

No one likes being wrong. For some people, admitting this can be an impossible feat even when they know it to be true in their hearts. I promise you—being wrong isn't the worst thing that can happen to you. I would make the argument that perpetual discontent and a lifetime of being unfulfilled are much, much worse.

The trouble with facing the you-don't-know-what-you-don't-know conundrum is...well...knowledge. This can create a multitude of "What if?" questions, and succumbing to those questions is an expert-killer. You start to realize how much went wrong because you went all in on someone else's beliefs. You start to understand how events and/or situations could have gone another way, maybe in a way that would have been more positive and better aligned with your wants and needs. The core truth is that you can only make decisions based on the information you have and the information you are open to receiving.

Let's talk about Santa Claus, the Easter Bunny and the Tooth Fairy for a minute. Whether or not you celebrate Christmas and Easter and your kids losing their baby teeth, you're likely familiar with the premise of each of these characters. You also know the dirty little secret about them: they aren't real. Everyone you know lied to you about Santa and the Easter Bunny and the Tooth Fairy for a number of years. When you found out about that lie, you probably became the next keeper of the secret because you had younger siblings or relatives and your family didn't want those magical characters spoiled for them. Your life didn't fall apart. You didn't run away from home because you realized that your parents had lied to you. Years later, you didn't wind up explaining to a significant other that finding out that Santa Claus didn't exist is why you can't trust people. You accepted what you didn't know, incorporated the new information and moved on.

But what if you heard that Santa, the Easter Bunny and the Tooth Fairy weren't real and you refused to consider that new information? Your family might have gone along with it for a while, but ultimately, if they couldn't convince you of the truth (especially once you reached adulthood), then you probably would have found yourself in a therapist's office.

That example is an oversimplification, but the general concept is a vital one to recognize if you want to be in charge of your own life. Beliefs are *not* fixed things unavailable for examination. Some beliefs are easy to reconfigure; others are much more difficult. Those hard-to-address beliefs usually center on situations where we don't feel like we are enough in some way or times when we're facing health challenges or times when we have unresolved emotions. In all of these cases, the underlying factor is fear.

When you read about my cancer diagnosis and my response to it, did you think I was crazy? Or did my story open your mind to alternative ways of dealing with health challenges (or doctors or the medical system)? Maybe you wondered what specifically made me so confident about my decision. Have you ever asked your own doctor for their success/failure statistics in relation to prescriptions and treatment protocols? Have you read any of the medication guides that accompany your prescriptions or looked at the studies pharmaceutical manufacturers submitted to the FDA? If none of those questions came up for you, ask yourself why they didn't.

Medical scenarios are just one example of the unfortunate fact that belief systems are tricky to deal with. Often, we aren't even aware that what we believe is limiting or mistaken in any way—we think of beliefs as rigid facts, not something subject to change or understanding differently. Most of our beliefs are imparted to us by others, usually in childhood. As we grow older, we naturally change some of those beliefs, but many stick. What generally happens is that we continue going round and round in an endless loop, stuck in systems of belief that don't serve us.

Such deeply-rooted, deeply-ingrained systems govern what we think of ourselves, others and life. These beliefs are often called "blocks." Here are some common examples of blocks:

- I don't have time.
- Life is supposed to be hard.
- Some people are just lucky.
- I can't afford what I want.

- I am a victim.
- If things are too easy, there must be a catch.
- My body is broken in some way and/or will inevitably attack itself.
- I'm not good enough.
- I'm not enough.
- It's better to go along to get along than express how I feel.
- I'm only important if other people approve of me and/or accept me.
- Change is hard.
- I can't do that.
- I can't be that.
- I can't become that.
- It must be nice to _____.
- I wish I could _____.

Blocks around health are some of the most difficult ones to unravel. In order to do so, it might be helpful to understand adaptation. That is the process of adjusting to new circumstances or factors, either in a positive or negative direction. Our bodies are *always* working to adapt to keep us alive, but our current lifestyles and environments are creating countless stressors, toxins and deficiencies that our bodies must contend with.

I invite you to consider this: what the Western medical world calls "illness" may just be adaptation. What if pain is a message? The message is that you've done too much or maybe that what you're doing isn't ideal under the current circumstances. Perhaps that pain is issuing you an invitation to change.

Your chronic anxiety, depression and poor mood are indicators that you've shifted your mind, body and spirit into a negative direction. Could that be an invitation to observe and reflect on your life and whom you choose to share it with? Those symptoms could be indicators of terrible relationships, toxicities and deficiencies or could be the result of chronically consuming negative media (TV, news, social media, etc.). In all of those cases, your chronic challenges could point the way to changing your life for the better.

If you're dealing with cancer, consider that a tumor could be the result of a walled-off poison, toxin or emotion. What if your body created a tumor because it couldn't immediately deal with something? Dealing with the root cause could prompt a tumor to resolve itself in a less detrimental way than what modern medicine may suggest doing. That tumor could be a wake-up call to shift your mindset in a positive direction, move your body and consume real food.

Perhaps you've admitted that you have no idea how your body works and that you've given control over your mind, body and spirit to someone else. What if you said, "I'm going to change that"? You could tell yourself, "I can learn about my body and apply what I learn to my experience." You could stop going along to get along and believe in yourself instead.

Adaptation is change. The only constant in this life is change. The quicker you make friends with change, the quicker your quality of life will level up. How you are in this moment is *not* fixed—at any moment, you can shift your focus, energy and awareness. You can adapt or survive in misery until you die. You can adapt or survive in wellness until you die. The choice is yours.

Your takeaway...

Your belief may be inaccurate or incorrect.

You don't know what you don't know.

Out of the book and into your life...

What if the beliefs that most people have about cancer are like the Easter Bunny and no one told you? How would you feel? How would knowing that change your life or the life of someone else?

This shift in thinking can be applied to any subject matter—take out the word "cancer" in the above question and insert whatever your challenge is.

Here are some examples to get you started.

What if the beliefs most people have about _____ are like the Easter Bunny and no-one told you?

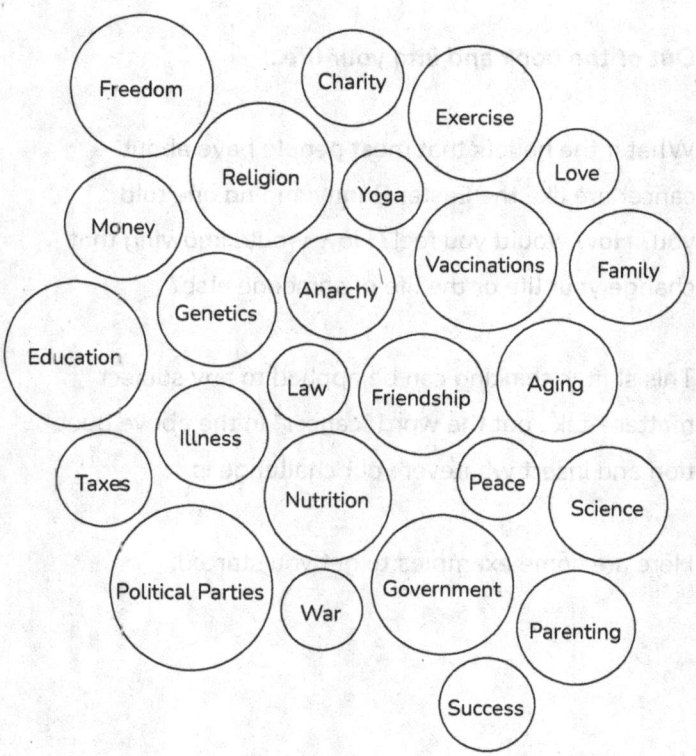

Freedom

Charity

Exercise

Religion

Yoga

Love

Money

Vaccinations

Family

Genetics

Anarchy

Education

Law

Friendship

Aging

Illness

Taxes

Nutrition

Peace

Science

Political Parties

War

Government

Parenting

Success

What feelings, thoughts, ideas, etc. came up for you during this exercise? Explore all of that a little bit more. Why did those come up? Why didn't they?

Think about what you're sure you know. Could that be wrong? Is it relevant? Can you accept and/or change your beliefs to have a life of true wellness?

Truth

"Facts do not cease to exist because they are ignored."
– Aldous Huxley

We all know that truth has a certain ring to it, a vibration. You know it when you hear it. Parents are fantastic at sniffing out lies from their children; people know when a friend isn't being truthful; partners tend to know when a significant other is lying. When we're faced with something that doesn't quite hit us right, we know. Often, that something pisses us off or shocks us. We don't need anyone else to tell us, not really. We just *know*.

In that moment of knowing, we make a choice: to accept what we know or willfully ignore it. When we choose to accept it, we are set on a path to get to the bottom of things. When we choose willful ignorance, we make excuses and give people the benefit of the doubt. We say to ourselves, "I know this isn't right, but I just can't deal with it" or "I don't want to deal with it." Or we might even think, "I will ignore this lie because I don't want to blow up my life."

But each time we opt for willful ignorance, we lose a little piece of ourselves. We set up a framework to draw in more undesired outcomes and give our power away. We create a foundation of fear that underpins our decision-making.

Fear is a tricky bastard. We are hard-wired for safety, yet the safe route is often the one that leaves us disillusioned, sad, lonely and unfulfilled. The safe route has us following someone else's idea of success. The rules of society dictate that things *should* be a certain way, that we can only claim success or wellness if certain criteria are met. That there are rules of behavior we must all live by to get what we want.

To acknowledge the truth of what we want and who we are is the only way out of a life based on fear and dictated by *shoulds*. Most people die full of regret because they willfully ignore this fact out of fear of the unknown. Living in fear makes us an easy target, and not in a good way. Evildoers can spot a target from a mile away because targets have their own vibration. The base note of that vibration is fear.

If you took a long, hard look in the mirror, would you see truth staring back? What pieces of yourself have you given away so as not to rock the boat?

We can't talk about truth without talking about information censorship. Here's a hard truth: if you don't want to read, listen to or watch something, then don't. But know that you do not have the right to keep whatever that is from others. Censorship is never acceptable! If that's hard for you to hear, ask yourself why you feel the need to control what others do. Really consider how getting so upset and bothered by other people affects you. When you find that answer, you'll also know how to improve other areas of your life. And you'll be on your way to true wellness.

When you're balanced energetically and emotionally, you

begin to realize that things like censorship are just distractions that will trip you up along the way. Consider the huge subject of health. If information is censored and you have a condition or disease, you're making decisions without having all the facts. Everything cutting-edge and new happens on the fringe. Does your doctor hang out on the fringe? No? Well, then you're making serious decisions without all of the available information.

Here's where *the quality of your questions determines the quality of your life*. It's important to evaluate whose opinions you trust, because people don't always have the same perspectives (or beliefs) that you do. Opinions are personal views and are subject to change anytime, for any reason, rational or otherwise. Opinions are not truth—opinions are beliefs, and beliefs aren't necessarily the truth, either. Trust and verify. You already do this with your kids, significant other, family and friends. Why aren't you doing it with doctors, lawyers, influencers, physical therapists, preachers, massage therapists, chiropractors, acupuncturists, life coaches, naturopaths and others in your life? Experts judge for themselves.

Your takeaway...

Truth has a resonance; you already know it.

Out of the book and into your life...

Make a list of three to five instances where you knew someone wasn't telling the truth. How did you know? Was it the tone of their voice or their body language? Did they give you conflicting information? Something else? Did you ignore your gut feelings/intuition?

Now think of three to five instances where you knew someone wasn't telling the truth but you willfully ignored it or decided that you just couldn't deal with it for whatever reason. How did things work out? Is that person still in your life? If so, what kind of relationship do you have? Did you ever think to yourself that you wished you hadn't ignored your gut feeling? Why or why not?

Fear

"He who has overcome his fears will truly be free."
– Aristotle

Have you ever asked, "What's stopping me?" I am absolutely positive that the answer is fear. This nasty one-syllable word can do a number on you. Whatever dreams you have tucked away in a hidden place are held at bay by the dark guard of fear.

- Fear of getting what you want (or not getting it).
- Fear of the unknown.
- Fear of gossips.
- Fear of rejection.
- Fear of love.
- Fear of failure.
- Fear of success.
- Fear of many variations of the above.

There are quite a few "helpers" out there who love to say that fear never goes away. I don't believe that's true. What you're afraid of and how intensely you experience fear can and will change.

Let's see if we can demystify fear. Do you remember learning how to ride a bike or swim? Maybe you initially did have some fear around learning those skills. However, once you began the process, the fear started to dissipate. That's because once you learn something, you aren't afraid of it anymore. *Knowledge beats fear.*

That said, fear can be useful. Being mindful of a hot burner while cooking is a healthy fear. You take precautions and avoid getting burned. Then again, some might say getting burned comes with the territory—the longer you use the stove, the more likely you are to get burned. Still, you use the stove. Even if you do get burned, the chance that you'll need medical attention is low.

And *that*, my friends, is how you deal with fear! The magic is in the doing. You have to *address* the thing you're afraid of and deal with it. Facing your fears means going *through* the process, not avoiding it.

Of course, stoves don't say unhelpful things to us as we're cooking on them, but all of the well-meaning and not-so-well-meaning people in our lives love to chime in! Sometimes strangers even get in on the action. You need to keep in mind that other people's thoughts about how you live and what you're doing don't actually threaten your safety. Not everyone—not even family and friends—is meant to be part of your everyday life for the duration.

People come and go. When you have clarity around yourself, your life, your wants and needs, you can *let* them go. That will be a welcome release when it comes to some people; letting others go will break your heart. But it's a necessary process, because allowing your circle to be filled with fearful, change-resistant people is contributing to why your life is not the way you want it to be. Some people are only meant to be part of your life in small doses. And by the way, you can have relationships with people who disagree with you! That might seem like a real shocker given the current state of the world, but basically, it's a matter of knowing who you are and just letting them be.

Essentially, if you want to be the expert of your life, you have to decide on the kind of people you want to be around daily and occasionally. Your group is either lifting you up or tearing you down. Folks who like to tear down others are running a fear program. *We all have the same calling and purpose: to be the best humans we can be by utilizing our unique perspectives, skills, talents and abilities as we move through life.* The *how* of doing so is what varies. If you are ignoring any of those perspectives or skills or talents or abilities for the sake of others, you will never get what you want. The same applies if you're choosing to surround yourself with fearful people.

If you're having trouble with any of the ideas in this book, fear is almost certainly the culprit. Fear gets in the way. It is *the* block, *the* obstacle. To be the expert of your life, everything you think, believe, want, need and understand must be on the table and up for discussion. That's how you grow and expand—there's no way around it. Some people will be with you; some won't. Your eyes will be opened to things that will make you think, "How could I not see this?"

It may feel like you're grieving the things you've left behind. You are. Your job is to feel the emotions and move through the stages of grief. Friends, family and strangers will call you crazy, attack you, criticize you...basically tear you down. They might do this to your face or behind your back. Others will say "Yes!" They'll be thankful that they've found a kindred spirit. The things you leave behind will be replaced with more of the things that light you up, make you happy and bring excitement into your world. There will be new friends, new teachers and so much more.

You can let fear be a distraction, or you can decide that enough is enough. Be gentle with yourself as you move through fear and get back to the business of being you. Peel back the layers of what doesn't serve you and discard those layers. It's called the "comfort zone" for a reason. Change doesn't happen there!

Discernment will help you know when to stay and when to go. You don't have to deal with all the challenges at once—start small and keep on keeping on. Losing any more of your life to fear of the unknown is a choice. You can choose to change the script!

Your takeaway...

Fear is the root cause of life's challenges. The only way out of fear is to go through it.

Out of the book and into your life...

Do something that's out of your comfort zone. It doesn't have to be a big thing—just pick something you wouldn't ordinarily do. Start exploring all of your interests that you've put on the back burner! See what I did there ;) Maybe do an activity you wouldn't typically do by yourself.

Afterwards, take 5 to 10 minutes to reflect on your experience. Did it turn out like you anticipated? What feelings were predominant before and then afterwards? Take note of anything that stands out to you. How easy would it be for you to do that activity again, to make doing new things a regular part of your life? If it doesn't feel like it would be easy, why not?

Credentials

"I can't give you a brain, but I can give you a diploma."
— L. Frank Baum

Opening your mind and keeping it open is the greatest gift you can give yourself. That's when you can heal, blast through obstacles and dissolve limiting beliefs. Please remember this: growing and expanding as a person happens more as a spiral than a straight line. You'll find yourself dealing with the same things again and again until they're truly resolved. Most of the time, growth and expansion happen in stages. That's how we obtain the space we need to process and integrate the knowledge and experience we gradually gain. Having an open mindset lets us reevaluate matters and consider what's right in front of us.

Here's where I challenge you to examine your filters (a.k.a. perspectives) on education, licensing and credentialing. Review the statements below and make note of your immediate reaction to them.

- Specialists are experts.
- College graduates are smarter than everyone else.
- Doctors of any kind are smarter than anyone else.
- Doctors are working for my best interests.
- State licensing ensures my safety.
- It's not acceptable for me to question any specialist, professional, doctor or expert.
- Someone's personal experience with a subject does not count as knowledge or wisdom on the topic.
- Receiving a certificate of any kind means that the recipient understands the information presented and how to apply it.

- I'm happy to accept without question what authorities of any kind say, do and tell me to do.

Now write down your answers to the questions below:

- What criteria do you use to select a medical professional?
- If you ask friends and family for referrals, what criteria does that person have that qualifies them to refer you to anyone?
- Do you know where the medical professional you're seeing went to school? Does that matter? Do you know whether they were at the top of their class or the bottom?
- Did you check with the state licensing board to see if they've had complaints or malpractice issues?
- Do you know if they own stock in any pharmaceutical companies? Yes, this is a real thing. Doctors can and do own stock in the companies that make the drugs they prescribe. While The Centers for Medicare & Medicaid Services maintains a publicly accessible database on this very topic, it is only a place to start. It is limited by the years available for search and the loopholes for disclosure. Be

sure to check out the Resources section at the end of the book for a link to the database and more information.

- Do you believe that your healthcare professional has your best interests at heart? Why or why not?
- Do you know whether or not they regularly read and study research?
- Do they refer you to acupuncturists, naturopaths, chiropractors, etc.?
- Does this professional listen to you and answer all of your questions? Pay attention to you for more than 5 to 15 minutes during your appointment? Or do they talk down to you?
- Have you asked this professional about any affiliations, kickbacks or other forms of payment they get for prescribing medications or treatments?
- Do you do your own research on any medications, protocols and/or treatments they recommend to you? Do you do your own research regardless of the topic?
- What about other professionals you interact with throughout your life? Does it matter where your accountant went to school? Whether or not they were at the top or bottom of their class? How

I'd be willing to bet that most of you don't ask even half of those questions, but it's imperative for you to understand that medical professionals *work for you*. You do not work for them. All professionals work for you. You've probably trusted your hairdresser or barber with more intimate details of your life than you've trusted your doctor with. That's because we tend to build up people who hold certain positions and put them on pedestals and above questioning. We think because they went through a rigorous education, that enables them to become experts on every patient they see. Mind you, this can happen in any field on any subject—it doesn't only apply to doctors.

Yes, some people are smarter than you. Some people are smarter than you regarding *certain things*. And some aren't smarter than you at all regardless of their credentials. The only expert of you is *you*! At the end of the day, all of these educated, licensed, credentialed professionals are only people. They should *never* be placed on a pedestal.

Choose any profession you'd like and fill in the blank: _____ **are people and people aren't perfect.**

Let's explore. College graduates aren't smarter than everyone else; people who didn't attend college aren't less smart than everyone else. You can be great at doing something and not great at sitting in a classroom. And when it comes to specialists, their view is so narrow that they can be truly awesome in one area yet oblivious about how something fits into the greater whole. In the field of healthcare, specialists can often get in the way of healing if they treat you like a machine with parts and they're only dealing with one of those parts. But humans are *not* machines—humans are interconnected, energetic beings. Even mechanics understand the parts are interconnected. You won't find a mechanic that says the battery is the most important part of the car and disregards every other part or system under the hood. What happens in your mind is reflected in your body and vice versa. What happens with one organ affects every other organ. Being a specialist without this understanding is a hindrance. If your health professional doesn't understand the importance of interconnectedness, fire them immediately.

Know that licenses, registrations, certifications and other credentialing methods do not keep you safe. At worst, they are money-making rackets and do not indicate ability or intellect. At best, they show that a minimum level of knowledge was attained. The person with that set of credentials might not have any understanding as to how that knowledge can be applied. Yes, this even applies to doctors!

Many state and private qualifications were designed to inhibit competition rather than guard consumer/patient safety. Do you really believe that your hairstylist or plumber would suddenly lose their skills if they failed to pay a licensing fee? What about your lawyer? Teachers? Massage therapists? Nurses? Real estate and insurance agents?

I'll use myself as an example of this. I hold a 200-hour yoga certification. When I completed this certification, I was told that I must register with the Yoga Alliance because that's how people would know I was a professional. I dutifully gave them my money and got permission to use RYT (Registered Yoga Teacher) after my name. And that was that. In almost 20 years of teaching, I've never had anyone ask me if I was registered with the Yoga Alliance. The only people who care about the RYT designation are other yoga teachers. That's because a unique money-making racket was created for and in the yoga world.

The topic of yoga is giant. You could spend your entire life studying just one area of it—take breath work, for instance. The physical practice is only a small part of the whole. Anyone can train other people to teach yoga. Some of these people are awesome; some are not. Some are part of the Yoga Alliance; some are not. Anyone can create an organization or association around any field. It may or may not lend credibility to that field.

Running a yoga studio successfully requires having a lot of bodies on the mats, and providing yoga teacher training is the most efficient way to keep the doors open. To make the math easy, let's say your drop-in rate for a class is $10 and all of your monthly bills for the studio are $1,000. That means someone needs to pay you $10 a hundred times each month. If your studio only holds 20 people at a time, how will you make enough money? By offering multiple classes seven days a week, having a store, giving workshops, even running a café alongside your studio— and providing teacher training. Many schools offer a few teacher trainings yearly, and *that's* what puts their business in the black. A 200-hour yoga teacher training package generally costs thousands of dollars. Staying with our example, let's say that 20 people sign up for teacher training at $3,000/person. These trainings are offered four times a year. That's a total of $240,000. (20 people x $3,000 per person = $60,000 per teacher training x 4 trainings per year = $240,000.) You can see how the potential to make a great deal of money could attract a certain kind of person.

Yoga teacher training is a relatively innocuous example of this kind of credentialing. Quality can and often does suffer when there's potential to make a lot of money in a relatively short amount of time. The first and the largest yoga studios in a given area will make the most money. That's why there are so many poor yoga teachers—the demand for teachers is not equal to the number of teacher training graduates. And that's also why this field is full of teachers who are simply regurgitators with no real understanding or integration of knowledge. You can likely think of similar scenarios in other fields.

Reclaiming your expert status requires evaluating information, including considering how valid credentials may or may not be. You are allowed to change your mind when new information comes to light. You need to! Information and knowledge invariably change, and our understanding of that new information and knowledge must also change.

Despite this, some doctors completely dismiss new information and fail to offer it to their patients.

Experts are 100% responsible for themselves. Experts do their own research. Experts never make a decision about anything without investigating all sides of a topic. After all, how could you possibly say you've done your due diligence if you didn't consider *all* of the information?

Experts don't know everything about everything, but they *do* know how to evaluate information and research and apply what they've learned. *Even if it goes against the mainstream.*

Your takeaway...

Experts trust themselves implicitly. Licenses, degrees and other credentials do not equal competency.

Out of the book into your life...

Consider what certificates, licenses, diplomas, etc. you blindly accept. Since these things are held by people and people aren't perfect, why are you blindly accepting their advice? You doubtless know quite a few people who are excellent cooks. They aren't, however, chefs. Because they do not have the designation of "chef," do you not partake in their culinary creations? Would you not consider taking culinary advice from them because they aren't officially "chefs"? Do *you* not cook at home because you lack the title of "chef"?

PART 4

LIBERATION

Undoing

"Every next level of your life will demand a different you."
— Inky Johnson

Reclaiming expert status usually doesn't happen overnight. It happens by degrees over time and with some occasional bigger leaps along the way. That's just as it should be, because everything you know to be true will come up for discussion. The undoing process is a process where you deprogram, unlearn and undo much of what you think and know. It's messy. It's scary. And it's completely worth it.

We are all products of how we were raised, who we learn from and what we consume. We aren't always as open as we could be. Consider parents and parenting. It's a sure sign of maturity to recognize that parents are people and people aren't perfect. Your parents did the best they could at the time. Most of us can say both good and bad things about our parents, with more items landing in one column than the other. But that truly makes no difference, because *you* are 100% responsible for your life. It doesn't matter who did what in the past or how good or bad things were then or how things are now. Whatever your situation is today, you are responsible for it.

You may very well have been a victim of something negative, horrible, violent and/or traumatic. While that will doubtless present you with obstacles, that doesn't change your level of responsibility. Making what happened your whole identity and living your life in that victimhood is a choice. That's not to say that choosing to be your own expert will be easy! I am not making light of horrendous experiences. But I am saying that each of us gets to choose how we show up. You can change how you show up in the world anytime, in any moment, in any way.

As a child, perhaps you were told "No!" and "You can't do that!" and "You'll never make a living that way!" Or maybe you were encouraged and supported, but that encouragement came from parents who thought you could do no wrong and who rewarded a lack of talent, skills and effort instead of creating teachable moments around being honest. Good parents have hard conversations about perfecting skills and talents and making an effort.

If you're a parent yourself, don't enable your kids' lack of talent, skill or effort. Be honest with your kids. Help them be better! What you teach your kids sets the tone for the rest of their lives. Often, we hear that kids are sponges, but it's more accurate to say that they're recorders—when they're young, kids are recording everything they see and hear. This recording becomes the software that runs their lives. It is their point of reference for how to do and be in the world.

As an adult, gaining an awareness of what you carry around from your upbringing and how it does or does not serve you is where your work starts. Yes, your parents laid the groundwork. If, however, parts of your life aren't working, *you* are responsible for fixing those parts.

List the pros that stem from your upbringing. What did you learn then that serves you now? Now list the cons. What did you learn then that does *not* serve you now? Do you think you're a victim of your childhood circumstances? If so, do you believe you can change your current circumstances? Think about your parents as being people with their own wants and needs that had nothing to do with being parents. Then think about how those potentially unfulfilled wants and needs may have manifested in your upbringing. If you're a parent yourself, have you lost yourself in the label of "parent"?

If your life is challenging and you aren't getting the results you want, there's a problem with the program you're running, namely that your beliefs and your experiences are not matching up. This is a great place to explore the concept of separating the message from the messenger. Have you ever heard the expression that a broken clock is right twice a day or that a blind squirrel occasionally finds a nut? Such expressions summarize what it means to separate the message from the messenger. By the same token, just because someone is occasionally correct or lucky doesn't make them experts over you. Again, results matter. And you're reading this book because you don't like your current results.

Time to separate the message from the messenger! If you really start to look at the people who are expressing opinions and offering advice about your life, you won't have to ask too many questions before the resonance of truth hits you like a ton of bricks. To use one example, do you have friends and family who are living paycheck-to-paycheck but are telling you how to run your business or plan for retirement? Take a long, hard look at them before deciding whether they have anything to offer that will help you get the results you want. Would you really use that broken clock to help you show up in a punctual manner?

A good way to find genuine experts is to find people who are living their talk. I'll admit that this isn't the easiest thing to do. It takes time, for one thing, partially because people living their talk aren't incessantly telling other people about it. They don't need to—the culmination of their words and actions are congruent. These people know a thing or two about deprogramming, unlearning and undoing. They know how to create what they want. They don't go around asking permission to do or be. They *are* their own experts. They know it. They live it.

You can do that, too! The beauty of life is that you can make yours be whatever you want it to be...*if* you're willing to tune in, listen to your gut and let go. Let go of the old programs you're running! Rigid rules regarding what constitutes happiness, success, creativity, etc. that do not serve you. You must take your power back and commit to a new way of being and doing.

Your takeaway...

Stop entrusting your life to people who can't do it themselves, whatever that "it" may be.

Out of the book and into your life...

Can you identify any programs or rules you're living by that don't reflect how you feel? Is there anything you do, practice or support that you only do because of your family and friends? If you did things your way, what would you gain? Would you lose anything?

Process

"If you quit on process, you are quitting on the result."
– Idowu Koyenikan

I like to think of the processes of dealing with challenges and working towards goals in the same way. The heart of doing both comes down to the following:

- Get your mind right
- Simplify
- Repeat

I realize this three-point plan sounds too good to be true, but hear me out. Generally, we are toting around so much baggage that we tend to make things much more difficult than they need to be. We're also fighting unhelpful programming we've picked up along the way and are living in fear. If you want to be well, create what you want, enjoy life and be content, then your first priority has to be to get your mind right. It cannot happen any other way.

Getting your mind right will be different for each person and situation. If you're dealing with health challenges and all you do is complain and talk about your symptoms and how sick you are, healing will be difficult. If you're in a situation where you are fearful and difficult decisions must be made, you'll likely make a bad one or miss out on finding what would actually help you.

To get your mind right, start asking yourself these questions: What do I need to be less fearful? How can I get the information I need to feel prepared for what I have to deal with? Make a list of everything you're afraid of, then start analyzing and evaluating that list. If you have doom-and-gloomers in your life, can you back away from them and tighten your circle? Can you identify thoughts and feelings that may be coming from others, things that don't align with your own opinions or beliefs? Question everything!

Next, consider what can you do right now to eliminate some stress. Maybe prep meals for the week, select outfits for the week, pack the gym bag the night before, hire someone to take over doing a task you hate, pack a lunch instead of eating out, etc. Simplify, then simplify again, then simplify again. Don't underestimate the power of simplicity!

We really need very little to be happy, healthy and fulfilled. Having a fear of missing out (FOMO), feeling like we have to keep up with the Joneses and feeling beaten down by other societal pressures tremendously skew things for us and create additional stress. This stress usually starts off as a minor thing, but when we aren't mindful and aware of ourselves and what we're thinking/feeling, that minor stress can easily turn into chronic stress. From there, it becomes something even bigger. This is a major contributing factor to most dis-eases, conditions and dis-orders.

Get super clear on what works for you and what doesn't,

even when it comes to something as basic as fashion. For example, although I would love to wear flowy dresses and tops, I avoid them like the plague because they're very unflattering to my shape. I realize that sounds like an utterly ridiculous example of simplifying, but it epitomizes how we live our lives: we resist and fight instead of accepting and adapting. Steve Jobs and Albert Einstein put their wardrobe on auto-pilot (they wore the same thing every day) to free up brain power to work on other things. As you look for ways to simplify your life, consider where you're always banging your head against the wall looking for something other than what you you've got. Can you just accept what you *do* have instead?

Lastly, repeat getting your mind right and simplifying. These three steps constitute the process. Reflect on all aspects of your life through the filter of The Five Challenges you read about in Part 2. That will help you figure out where to start and how to accept your whole self: your mind, body and spirit. This is how you become the expert of your life and claim 100% responsibility for it. With your expert status, you'll then do whatever is necessary to create what you want.

The process for getting where you want to go gets easier each time you move through it. You'll make decisions much more quickly because you'll know that if something doesn't align with your core values, you're out. The answers come from inside.

The process to get the results you want in life won't be the same with each idea, goal or vision you have. Your core values can change depending on your current priorities. For me, freedom over my time has become so integral to what I want that it's largely a non-negotiable for me. That doesn't mean there aren't times when I'm super busy with little time to spare, but it does mean that such periods of busyness are directly related to whatever priority is at hand and the overarching value of having freedom over how I spend my time. Those core values will be different for everyone—depending on yours, for example, practical considerations may rule supreme in a particular situation.

Spend some time getting some clarity over who you are, what you want/need and the action steps you're willing to take. We all have areas of our life that come naturally and easily to us, areas we already know how to move through. When something doesn't come easily and fear dominates, everything we want seems out of reach. But here's the thing: *if you can get what you want in one area of life, you can get it in all areas of your life.* The universe loves clarity and focus. Without clarity and useful focus, though, you may find part of what you want but not exactly what you want.

The best way to think of this process is making a shift in your thinking. *Everything* begins and ends with your mindset! You can pursue endless possibilities and techniques for opening up your mind. As you experiment, you'll find some go-to methods that work for you and others that you rotate through only as needed. Just committing to honestly answering the questions in this book will likely change your life and your level of awareness. Trust in the process, because *you* are driving the process. *You* are the expert.

Critical thinking is really what this is all about. If you let your results be your guide, then you're applying the components of critical thinking. The same applies to embracing the easy, natural, flowing parts of your life. You'll move through the following steps:

- Observation
- Analysis
- Interpretation
- Reflection
- Evaluation
- Inference
- Explanation
- Problem-solving
- Decision-making
- Adaptation/adjustment

When moving through challenges, it's hard to remember that we already have everything we need to arrive at the solution. Here are some questions to consider when you're stuck, when things aren't going your way, when you're processing experiences with the people in your life and/or when you're having trouble making a decision:

- What am I choosing between?
- What's my goal?
- What are the possibilities?
- What are the pros?
- What are the cons?
- How does the choice align with my values? Are

there any non-negotiables?

- What choice gets me closer to my goal?
- Who's involved with the situation/said something about it?
- Is that person an authority/expert or someone in a power position and does that matter?
- If any opinions or facts were given and any information omitted (purposely or not), was that done to help or hurt me?
- Did I have a public/private or written/verbal conversation with the people involved?
- Were those people open to questions and/or different perspectives?
- What was their emotional state like when they said whatever they said?
- Do I truly care about that person's opinion?

Your takeaway...

The process for applying the information in this book
is 1) Get your mind right, 2) Simplify, 3) Repeat.

Out of the book and into your life...

The process is the journey. Keep coming back to these
three steps, asking yourself questions and honestly
reflecting on your answers.

Optimize

*"You don't get any points in life
for doing things the hard way."*
– Tim Fargo

When you're the lead (a.k.a. expert) of your own life, you understand that balance does not mean giving equal attention to every aspect of your life at the same time. Imagine standing on one leg. Even though you can't step forward, you're still able to breathe and your vision still functions and you still can talk and do so much more. That's essentially what a balanced life is. Even though your main focus might be on a particular area at a particular time, everything in the background doesn't just fall away. You can focus on standing on one leg without the rest of your body ceasing to function.

Is each area of your life working for you in the best way possible? If the answer is no, start evaluating and observing and asking questions. Maybe you don't need to do your absolute best in one area—you can just get the job done. Or maybe you need to tend to it immediately. Or maybe you can let it rest for a while.

Even though being able to balance our lives is a crucial skill, as children, most of us were not taught how to truly take care of ourselves. We were given food and clothes and shelter and taught what's polite and appropriate in society and what gets us shamed. But we didn't learn that the foundation of taking care of ourselves rests in the knowledge that the most important person in our lives is *us*. Not our children, not our friends or significant other or family or boss, etc. I realize this might sound a little harsh; stay with me.

Why is it so important to put ourselves first? Life is all about connection. Your connection with yourself is the foundation for how you connect with others. When you avoid your unresolved issues or give away your whole self to maintain a false ideal, your foundation is incomplete. Destroying yourself for the sake of others is not an admirable act. If you can't or won't deal with your issues, how will you teach your children to deal with theirs? What kind of job satisfaction or personal life will you have if you have zero boundaries with your employer? Maybe it's been so long since you charged your own batteries you don't know how. If you want to deeply connect: be seen, be heard and acknowledged then you must look in the mirror, listen to your inner voice and deal with what you find. From there, you will find purpose, meaning and how to be of service to the people in your life.

Have you actually become the best person you can be, or are you still living for the latest drama? Does scrolling through or living on social media make you feel jealous or angry? Or sad or upset, give you needed attention? By all means, feel what you feel! I'm not advocating for avoiding feelings, but I *am* advocating for not purposely causing ourselves to have negative feelings.

Too often, we ignore what we're feeling and continue in the same old way, not really dealing with life. We have children and live vicariously through them instead of getting a life of our own. We give those kids so much of ourselves that there's nothing left. Some of you already know what happens when those kids grow up: you have nothing of your own, so you keep chasing your kids around. The problem is that they're adults while you still want them to need you the way they did when they were five. Many of you will get divorced, because without children to deal with, you have nothing to share with your spouse.

But there is another way! *All you have to do is choose it.* Everyone shows up for the things they actively choose. The key to being the lead in your own life—the expert of your own life—is to *choose yourself.*

When you change your mind, you change your life. Growth begins when you stop accepting the status quo. Set down the weight of past expectations and step courageously into a new future! Revolutionize your attitude, blast through obstacles and claim your power. You are limitless. Take a small step. Little movements add up! The more you do, the more you *can* do. Breathe deeply.

Reflect. Tell your inner kid, you know the one with the head full of doubt, that everything is ok. You were always enough! Create space for a new version of you, one who does not need permission to shine.

Dive into motion. Embrace new ideas, run towards opportunities, choose the path that calls to you. Reach for results that *you* define and don't ever settle for just "good enough." Your story is yours to write, and at any moment, you can twist the plot and change the ending.

Break through. Leaders go first. Trust your intuition, step past the rules, celebrate adventure. You have one beautiful chance to choose anything you want, so pick your own damn self. After all…

You are the expert.

PART 5

EXPLORATION

Research

"Always do your own research."
– experts everywhere

As you make your way along the path to wellness, it's also necessary to understand the nuance of research studies and their use/misuse of statistics. Doing your own research seems to challenge numerous belief systems, but it's a necessary process. Time to jump into often-overlooked details!

When it comes to medical studies, the gold standard for research is the double-blind, independent study. That's because such a study eliminates or reduces conflicts of interest, impropriety, the placebo effect and bias with both doctors and patients . To explore this concept, let's say that I'm the owner of a pharmaceutical company and I pay for my own research. The experiments that make up that research are facilitated and conducted by my company. In each experiment, we use only ten subjects.

On the surface, there's nothing wrong with this scenario. Ideally, once the experiment has been completed, I would publish an article informing the scientific community of my findings. Then, *without my involvement*, an independent team would use my methods and parameters to see if the results my company got could be duplicated. If the exact same results under the exact same conditions are not obtained, then my study is thrown out. If my results *are* the same as the independent results, then my premise is considered to be a sound one. If the results are similar but not exactly the same, then further debate and study are needed.

Conducting a double-blind, independent study is obviously a time-consuming process, but *not* following this orderly process opens the door to grave misunderstandings and is used by some without integrity to increase their wealth. Most concerningly, *not* following this careful process could result in unnecessary deaths.

Science as a field exists in flux. It is not set in stone; ideas are always up for debate, study and experimentation. There is no research that applies to 100% of people, 100% of the time. It can apply to the majority of people but in a study that could be 51% or 99%. This difference in *majority* can represent any number of people; from dozens to millions depending on the context. And in terms of the statistics used when stating results, those can unfortunately be manipulated—information can be perceived in a multitude of ways that either aren't accurate or give the illusion of something else. In particular, statistics can imply that a study involved more participants than it actually did. Obviously, a greater number of participants means more reliable results. Would you rather base your decision about taking a drug/pursuing a treatment on a study of thousands of people or ten people?

Let's keep going with our hypothetical example. Imagine

that my experiment involving a potential new drug has a 20% chance of improving your life. Therefore, it has an 80% chance of *not* improving your life. Here are a number of ways the same numbers can be stated:

- 2 out of 10 people had some improvement in their life
- 8 out of 10 people had no improvement in their life
- 20% experienced improvement
- 80% experienced no improvement
- 2/10 showed improvement
- 8/10 showed no improvement

If 80% showed no improvement, does that mean their life is utterly unchanged? What if "no improvement" means no improvement of the condition trying to be treated… but the participants were paralyzed after taking the drug? Paralysis is not an improvement. What if 80% died? Death is not an improvement.

And as far as the 20% of the "improved" participants are concerned, what if the improvements were minimal? For example, if a patient typically had symptoms 7 days a week but instead experienced symptoms only 6 days a week while on the drug, is that significant? Perhaps the reduction was for a minor symptom like a scratchy throat instead of a major symptom like migraines. What if everyone can't agree on the definitions of "major" and "minor" symptoms and what genuine relief looks like?

The point of reading a study is to find out the techniques, parameters and other pertinent details of that study. That information provides the context behind the statistics. A number in isolation tells you very little. I would definitely not make life-or-death decisions based on a non-contextualized number. And if the numbers and research were provided by the same company that created the drug, I wouldn't use that for decision-making, either. No business is going to tell you something bad about their products. An ethical company would want independent research to be done and would use that research to promote their products.

Some people say that following the money and questioning science and experts is something that only conspiracy theorists do. But if you aren't allowed to question any professionals, experiments, experts, companies, etc., then you've already lost control over your life. Unearthing someone's motivations for how they interact with you, whether or not they give you all of the relevant information and how they select the information they *do* give you are all wise actions to take. Research and science rely on questioning.

You *must* do your own research! The people whose opinions, recommendations and information you trust must be open to discussion about what they're telling you. Especially when it comes to healthcare, do not entrust your life to someone who wants to dictate to you rather than have an open conversation with you. You need to be sure that whatever professional you consult is working hand in hand *with* you, not talking *down* to you or favoring a course of action that benefits the provider financially.

Meditation

"With meditation, you become a sensitized super hero, completely in control with endless possibilities at your fingertips."
– Tara Stiles

The following information is meant to get you thinking, exploring and practicing. You can come back to these prompts again and again if you'd like—they aren't a one-and-done kind of thing. Depending on the area of your life you're exploring, you may want/need to revisit the prompts often.

I invite you to approach the following with an open mind and not fight whatever comes up for you. Instead, see if you can let the ensuing thoughts and emotions simply move through you. Think of this as an opportunity to meditate or reflect on your life—give yourself time to see what you see and let the truth of what you're experiencing come through, however profound or possibly messy it might be. You can use the numbered meditations individually or in any combination that works for you.

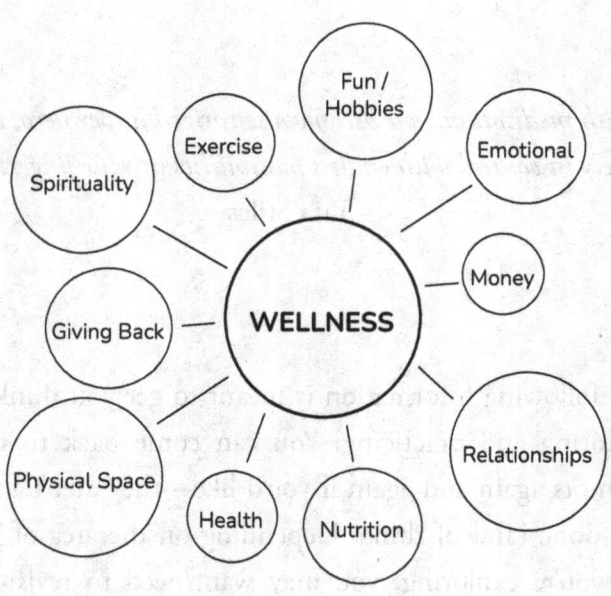

As you look at the image, consider which of these areas feel challenging and which feel easy. Which areas in your life might need attention? (You saw a similar exercise Part 2: Philosophy.)

All aspects of life don't and won't (and can't) get equal attention all of the time, nor will every area get 100% of your time, energy and attention. Because circumstances rarely stay the same, balancing your life involves movement. The inherent difficulty of such movement stems from whether you're *reacting* to or *responding* to life. You'll also need to define/redefine the beliefs you have around what balance means to you.

Ask yourself the following and see what comes up for you:

- What does this situation remind me of?
- Where does the "little girl" or "little boy" inside of me show up?
- Am I being honest about the situation?
- Have I acknowledged my fear and made a plan to deal with it?
- Have I acted on that plan?
- Am I forcing or grasping or holding on too tightly?

- Am I removed or distant? Or something else?
- What's one small thing I could do today that would help me feel better/deal with the challenges I'm experiencing and shift my mindset?
- What if how I think about stress is wrong?
- Does the word "stress" even mean anything to me?
- What if every difficulty, problem, challenge, disease, condition and/or illness is just a type of stress?
- What if I thought of that difficulty as a physical, chemical or emotional stress?
- What if I thought of the root cause of stress as being a toxicity or deficiency?
- Am I thinking critically and objectively in this situation?
- What does living in alignment with my core values look like?
- What does living in health and wellness look like?
- Do I know everything there is to know about this situation or person? Is there something I'm not considering? Do I have a blind spot on this issue? Is there something I'm avoiding or won't accept?

Meditation Moment #1

"When cleaning a room, it often gets messy before
it gets orderly. The same is often true for cleaning
your mind. So be patient and persevere with your
own journey. The only way out is through."
– Neil Strauss

In what ways or areas could you be more patient? More
patient with yourself? With others?

How might you help your family be more patient with
themselves and others?

How will patience help each of us improve our lives and
deal with all of our recent and future challenges?

Meditation Moment #2

"You can tell a person's mindset by
the shit they're impressed by."
– @healinguide

As you move through the healing journey, it's good to periodically reassess and reevaluate. Consider this: you are who you hang around. How might you tighten your circle? Do you spend your time with energy vampires or do you spend your time with people you can learn from or who raise the vibration of the room? Who might you let go of or at least adjust your boundaries with? Who might you invite into your life?

Meditation Moment #3

"FEAR has two meanings: 'Forget Everything And Run' or 'Face Everything And Rise.' The choice is yours."
– Zig Ziglar

Does anything currently cause you fear? Are you holding on to that fear? Have you found a tool for moving through that fear? If not, consider what you really want and need in this moment. What action step can you take to get it? How might taking action move you through your fear?

Meditation Moment #4

"And every day the world will drag you by the hand, yelling, 'This is important!

You need to worry about this…and this…and this!'
And each day it's up to you to yank
your hand back, put it on your heart and say
'No! *This* is what's important.'"
– Iain Thomas

If everything is important, then nothing is important. How do you/can you prioritize yourself? How might you take better care of yourself? Are you actually clear on what's important to you? Do you live that? How do you show your friends and family that you care for them? Where's your phone when you're at home? Are you chronically scrolling and responding to texts and emails?

If you are a caretaker or are dealing with a chronic disease or illness yourself, do you have a plan in place for how life might look in the future? Will you modify your schedule, including work and other responsibilities? Will you get help and delegate tasks? How can you include your family, kids, etc. in the process? Perhaps there are areas where they can take more responsibility. Are you making time just for you and for you and your partner?

Meditation Moment #5

"Every next level of your life
will demand a different you."
– Inky Johnson

It's time to celebrate, my friend! Look how far you've come! Take a moment and reflect on where you've been, what you've learned and how you've changed. Today, you are a new you.

Meditation Moment #6

"The body achieves what the mind believes."
– Anonymous

Stop! Inhale…slowly. Exhale. Repeat.

What have you been telling your body today? Your cells are listening. What beliefs do you have about your body today and healing in general? Have they changed recently? Why or why not?

Meditation Moment #7

"Appreciation: if we don't receive, we block flow.
Flow is like breathing in and out. If you only give and
never receive, it's like exhaling but never inhaling.
You'll feel burnt out and used or like no one cares for
you, only what you can do for them.
Receiving is the second part of true connection.
You connect with the world and it keeps you alive when
you inhale. You connect with other people and it keeps
your connection alive when you receive."

– Doe Zantamata

What (or who) do you appreciate today? Have you opened
yourself up to receive? If you haven't, why not? If you have,
is opening up a change from your normal behavior? What
have you learned from your new connections? How do
your new friends differ from the people you generally connect with?

Meditation Moment #8

"Don't stay faithful to who you used to be."
– Kain Ramsay

What are you holding on to from the past? Can you let it go? *Will* you let it go? Where are you allowing other people to define you? Perhaps you're still giving your energy to someone or something that no longer aligns with who you've become. What does it mean to be faithful to who you *used* to be rather than to your current self? Is what you're getting filling you up or draining you?

Meditation Moment #9

"Setbacks create comebacks."
– Les Brown

When you hear the words "setback," "obstacle," "challenge," "mistake" or "failure," what do you think? Is there any part of your life that you can use as the foundation for a comeback? Are mistakes and failures jamming you up? Imagine taking the lessons you've learned and integrating those into your life; imagine telling the story of when you used a setback to create a comeback. What if you saw hardship as an experience meant to teach you something instead of as a failure?

Meditation Moment #10

"I am the expert of my life and I am
100% responsible for it."
– Leslie Gilbert

Are you responsible for your life, or are you blaming others for what's happening? Are you playing the victim? Have you given your power away? Maybe you keep looking outside of yourself for an answer, *the* answer. Why? Is there anything you're avoiding? Are you willing to take full responsibility for your part in how you got here?

Meditation Moment #11

"My body is a reflection of my mind,
and my mind is a reflection of my body."
– Leslie Gilbert

Are you able to thank your body for any challenges? Try telling your body, "Thank you for getting me here, for your strength and resiliency." Try loving your body today. Meditate on the following: What if you thanked your body? What would you say? What emotions come up for you? Go deeper than surface level.

Resources

The following selected resources have been an integral part of my wellness journey. I have benefited greatly from these individuals' unwavering pursuit of life and work on their terms. #LeadersGoFirst!

As you consider these (and other) resources, keep in mind that you don't have to agree with everything someone says to learn from them.

Every effort has been made to ensure accuracy of the websites, social media links and other information. I do not receive (and haven't received) compensation for these recommendations.

Books

A Guide to Better Movement by Todd Hargrove, CR, CFP

Atlas Shrugged by Ayn Rand

Becoming Supernatural by Dr. Joe Dispenza

Hamer: A Critical Look at Healthcare by Mark Hanley

Letting Go: The Pathway of Surrender
by David R. Hawkins, M.D., Ph.D.

Mindset: The New Psychology of Success
by Carol S. Dweck, Ph.D.

Power vs. Force: The Hidden Determinants of Human Behavior by David R. Hawkins, M.D., Ph.D.

The Alchemist by Paulo Coelho

The Biology of Belief by Bruce Lipton, Ph.D.

The Fountainhead by Ayn Rand

The Four Agreements by Don Miguel Ruiz

The PH Miracle for Cancer: Discover the Truth about the Cause, Prevention, Treatments, and Reversal of ALL Types of Cancers by Robert Young DSc, Ph.D., N.D.

The Tao of Pooh by Benjamin Hoff

What Really Makes You Ill? Why Everything You Thought You Knew About Disease Is Wrong by Dawn Lester and David Parker

Why Zebras Don't Get Ulcers by Robert M. Sapolsky

You Can Heal Your Life by Louise Hay

Articles and other links

"How Your Mindset Determines Your Health"
https://www.bbc.com/future/article/20180410-how-your-mindset-determines-your-health

"Overdiagnosis and Overtreatment in Cancer: An Opportunity for Improvement"
https://jamanetwork.com/journals/jama/article-abstract/1722196

"National Cancer Institute Report Admits Millions have been falsely treated for 'cancer'"
https://www.naturalnews.com/042789_National_Cancer_Institute_false_treatments_misdiagnosis_epidemic.html

From the Editors of Lancet: "Medical Research is Unreliable at Best or Completely Fraudulent"
https://www.drugawareness.org/editor-of-lancet-medical-research-is-unreliable-at-best-or-completely-fraudulent/

From the Editors of Lancet: *"Half of Science is Wrong. An Underestimate?"*
https://www.wmbriggs.com/post/16092/

"Risky Drugs: Why the FDA Cannot Be Trusted"
https://ethics.harvard.edu/blog/risky-drugs-why-fda-cannot-be-trusted

"The Growing Problem of 'Fake Science"
https://www.dailysignal.com/2017/05/09/growing-problem-fake-science/

The Centers for Medicare & Medicaid Services maintains a publicly accessible database of payments that reporting entities—including drug and medical device companies—make to covered recipients like physicians. This database can be accessed at https://openpaymentsdata.cms.gov/.)

"Doctors Prescribe More of a Drug If They Receive Money from a Pharma Company Tied to It"
https://www.propublica.org/article/doctors-prescribe-more-of-a-drug-if-they-receive-money-from-a-pharma-company-tied-to-it

"Is Your Doctor Getting Drug Kickbacks?"
https://www.thehealthyhomeeconomist.com/is-your-doctor-getting-drug-kickbacks/

"Docs Paid Thousands to Promote Drugs They Prescribe"
https://www.nbcchicago.com/news/local/doctors-prescription-drugs/2055530/

"How to tell if your doctor is being paid to steer you to certain drugs"
https://clark.com/insurance/doctor-being-paid-steer-you-certain-drugs/

"Doctors Like to Think Big Pharma Doesn't Sway Them. It Does."
https://www.bloomberg.com/opinion/articles/2018-10-04/doctors-often-don-t-see-conflict-of-interest-in-drug-company-cash#xj4y7vzkg

"Doctors' financial interests, and potential conflicts, have become public information"
https://www.startribune.com/doctors-financial-interests-and-potential-conflicts-have-become-public-information/302311181/

Podcasts

Alfacast – Dr. Barre Lando and Mike Winner host some the of the most cutting-edge guests. Their show covers a wide range of topics: sustainable living, health and wellness, cryptocurrency, any subject that lands at the intersection of science and spirituality, and so much more. This podcast will certainly challenge your beliefs.
https://www.alfavedic.com/alfacast/

Dave Asprey – Dave Asprey explores the multitude of ways that technology can be applied to wellness.
https://podcasts.apple.com/us/podcast/the-human-up-grade-with-dave-asprey-formerly/id451295014

Extreme Health Radio – Justin and Kate Stellman interview wellness leaders from across the globe, all while sharing their lives (raising twins!) with their listeners. No topic is off-limits. You'll find a wide variety of experts on their shows. Great place to find some out-of-the-box thinkers.
https://www.extremehealthradio.com/

The Life Stylist – Luke Storey has no qualms about sharing all of the good and bad times in his life while also interviewing the movers and shakers of the wellness world.
https://www.lukestorey.com/lifestylistpodcast/

London Real – Brian Rose focuses on personal transformation and freedom and shares a wide variety of views and perspectives in these areas. You've likely heard of many of his guests, but you'll be pleasantly surprised by others.
https://londonreal.tv/

One Radio Network – Long-time radio host Patrick Timpone is your guide on this health and wealth podcast. This show is best described as a laid-back chat with friends.
https://oneradionetwork.com

Social Media Channels

Daniel G. Amen, M.D. @doc_amen
Dr. Amen has personally studied tens of thousands of brain scans all with mission to end mental illness and improve brain health. The amount of information regarding brain health available through his work is monumental.
https://www.instagram.com/doc_amen/

Sarah E Duvall, DPT, CPT @drsarahduvall
This mom of two brings a whole lot of heart and soul to her work in women's health. She's a pro at blending science and practicality. She is a breath of fresh air in her field and quite the athlete.
https://www.instagram.com/drsarahduvall/

Dr. Cassie Huckaby @dr.cassiehuckaby
After hitting a brick wall with allopathic medicine, Dr. Huckaby decided to follow her intuition and found her own way to healing. Armed with her mantra, "Your life is your medicine." she uses her natural medicine practice to help others transform their lives.
https://www.instagram.com/dr.cassiehuckaby/

Tommy John III @tommyjohniii
This guy is a unicorn in wellness world. He truly understands that degrees and other credentials mean nothing if
you don't know how to apply information to get results.
To illustrate that point, there's even a video of him
destroying his degree online. Don't let his directness and
frequent use of the F-word deter you. He is a wealth of
knowledge in healing and performance.
https://instagram.com/tommyjohniii

Perry Nickelston @StopChasingPain
After recovering from a back injury he devoted his work
to helping people get to the root cause of their pain and
heal.
https://instagram.com/stopchasingpain

Gary Vaynerchuk @garyvee
Gary is full of swear words and simple advice. He's a
great source for encouragement and finding out simple
ways that you can take action in your life and get over
yourself. He cuts to the heart of mindset work with zero
fluff.
https://instagram.com/garyvee

Websites

John Bergman, D.C.
Want to learn how your body works? Start here. Dr.
Bergman became a chiropractor after healing severe injuries (including a fractured sternum and skull, two broken legs and multiple organ damage) from an auto accident.
He taught anatomy, physiology and biomechanics for many years. He makes all of those subjects fun and easy to understand.
https://www.youtube.com/channel/UC8RPuonNxq2lM-b8zMvo7Xxw
Here's a great one to get you started, Chronic Disease Solutions. https://odysee.com/@MakingWiseTheSimple:b/bergman-chronic-disease:4

Atom Bergstrom
Atom has lived many lives in his 80+ years. He is a wealth of information on multiple subjects as he has dedicated decades of his life to research and integration. He is truly a wildly unique soul in the wellness world that will challenge all of your beliefs.
https://www.sunsyncnutrition.com/

Gregg Braden
Scientist, author, speaker, educator and visionary, Gregg
Braden has gone "all in" on human potential.
https://greggbraden.com/

Thomas Cowan, M.D.
Dr. Cowan is a well known voice against the mainstream
medical narrative. His book *Human Heart, Cosmic Heart:
A Doctor's Quest to Understand, Treat and Prevent Cardio-
vascular Disease* explains his paradigm shifting work on
why your heart is not a pump.
https://drtomcowan.com/

Jennifer Daniels, M.D.
Dr. Daniels is a long-time proponent of natural healing.
She has quite a story around applying the philosophy
results matter to her medical practice. She is a practical,
no nonsense resource that has strong opinions (based on
her own experiences) about Western medicine.
https://vitalitycycles.com/

Joe Dispenza, D.C.
Dr. Joe has a gift for bringing together people who feel in
their hearts, there is more to our world than we know but

aren't quite sure what to do with it. Much of his work involves bridging technology with the practice of meditation and how it impacts your life.
https://drjoedispenza.com/

Lee Holden
Holden has been helping people through Qi Gong for thirty years. He is a master at showing you how to tune in and how to apply the principles of this energy practice. He's laid-back, entertaining and makes it fun.
https://www.holdenqigong.com/

Wim Hoff
Hoff's story is a great lesson in the power of your mind and body. Proper breathwork alone can shift so many symptoms and emotions. He is a great guide to take you on that adventure.
https://www.wimhofmethod.com/

Jaiya John
I love this man's writing so much. His words feel like music to me and have such depth that each time you read them you're uncovering another layer of yourself.
https://jaiyajohn.com/

Andrew Kauffman, M.D.
Dr. Andy is a forensic psychiatrist, researcher, inventor and natural health consultant. He quit his thriving medical career to educate the world on viral theory. His work on viruses might take you through another mindset shift.
https://andrewkaufmanmd.com/my-story/

Bruce Lipton, Ph.D.
I love his book and it's a great read. I love his media appearances so much more. When you hear him speak, there's no denying his zest for life and sharing his work. He is regularly interviewed about his books and research. I found him very early in my journey. He has had a profound impact on my life. I'm not sure my book would exist without him. His work is a monumental mindset shift.
https://www.brucelipton.com/
Here's a quick video intro on The Biology of Belief.
https://www.youtube.com/watch?v=R4i2DRQFs7A
The full interview can be found here.
https://odysee.com/@freefromcensorship:7/Bruce-Lipton---Biology-of-Belief---London-Real:c

Richard Maybury

Maybury is a free market writer with a lifetime of real world experience. During his time in the United States Air Force he was a part of the 605th Special Operations Squadron. He also worked extensively with the CIA's School of the Americas in operations against Che Guevara. He shares his insights through his newsletter *Early Warning Report,* the "Uncle Eric" series of books and as a guest speaker on various podcasts.

www.richardmaybury.com/

Joseph Mercola, D.O.

A very thorough author, researcher, presenter and practitioner, Dr. Mercola has worked his entire career sharing his passion for treating the whole person not just their symptoms.

https://www.mercola.com/

Ron Paul, M.D.

Lifetime freedom and liberty advocate, Paul is the real deal. He has lived his talk his entire life. You'll find him discussing and analyzing current events and financial topics through his show Ron Paul Liberty Report.

https://odysee.com/@RonPaul:d

Kain Ramsay
Founder of Acology, Kain Ramsay has gained a huge
following through his straight forward, in depth training
programs. He is a fantastic story teller and uses that skill
to help people reflect on their own lives and/or as a coach
for others. He takes big topics and masterfully arranges
them into bite sized chunks that move you forward.
https://kainramsay.com/

Melissa Sell, D.C.
Dr. Sell is a Health Mindset Coach that focuses on
German New Medicine (Germanic Healing Knowledge).
Everything that ails you either is emotional or has an
emotional component. She helps you dig into all of that.
https://www.drmelissasell.com/

Mark Sisson
Mark is a former endurance athlete and founder of
Primal Blueprint. He has published a daily blog for years
and is a total pro on nutrition, fitness and wellness. As a
critical thinking researcher, he easily breaks down these
subjects.
https://www.marksdailyapple.com/

Tara Stiles
Tara is a revolutionary in yoga world. If she wasn't the first, she was one of the first to create *Yoga For* videos on YouTube. If you want down-to-earth yoga without all of the rules, dogma and guru based dynamics; you'll love Tara. She shares her work on finding ease through her podcast and Strala Yoga app.
https://www.tarastiles.com/

Chris Wark
Chris is another great example of someone listening to their gut and healing their own way. He embraced both medical intervention and a more holistic lifestyle to deal with his cancer diagnosis. Now, he has dedicated his life to sharing what he learned on that journey.
https://www.chrisbeatcancer.com/

Acknowledgments

Patrick... without you the story would be so different. For all of the times my heart said "yes" but my mind said "no" — thank you for nudging me forward.

Ryan and Trishy... thank you for sharing your journey with me. I am honored by your trust. Every chat that turned into deep conversations and every text message has forever changed me. I carry each of you in my heart.

Christy... even though you aren't here to buy the first copy like you wanted, your drive-by hugs are infused in these pages. Your friendship and support brightened my world. You are greatly missed sweet friend. Thank you!

Ashleigh, Janice, Ryan and Trishy... I am deeply appreciative of the time, consideration and feedback you offered as the first readers of this book. You eased a first time author into a new world.

Greg May... best advice ever! My journey started with you,

although, I could only see it in hindsight. I am forever grateful.

Lisa Howard... you helped me put two decades of my life into these pages. Your attention to my message and your willingness to work with a total newbie has made this experience so much better than I could have imagined. From the bottom of my heart, thank you.

Kristen O'Connell... I had so many questions. Thank you for your extreme patience in answering each one. You really helped take away so much stress while I navigated this process.

Arjan van Woensel... you had me at "Book Sherpa". When embarking on a challenging journey, great guides are essential. Thank you for your guidance. Keep walking on sunshine!

To all the people along the way... whether our time together was a lesson or a blessing I wouldn't change a thing.

About the Author

Leslie Gilbert is a Georgia based wellness practitioner, natural health researcher and yoga teacher. Through continual study, practice and education, Leslie healed herself from a multitude of symptoms and conditions. Armed with almost two decades of know-how in: breath-work, meditation, mindset and movement specialties; Leslie shares her knowledge and experiences to aid others in forging personal empowerment to create healthier and more fulfilling lives. You Are The Expert is her first book.

Write A Review

You, dear reader, are what's it all about! I love hearing what you have to say and I appreciate your feedback. Your input helps improve future editions and works.

By leaving a review on Amazon you help people make a better decision in their choice of book. Please go to https://tinyurl.com/leave5star today and let others know what you thought of *You Are The Expert*.

You, dear reader, understand all about how boring what you're interested in and appreciate your feedback. You forget the principle behind it and so work.

by reviewers here on Amazon and to help people make their best decision in their choice of book. If you go to buy a book, I know I would say I am glad I did and don't know what to do in the light in the book itself.

9 798987 306321